UNDERSTANDING W.S. MERWIN

HIX, H. L

UNDERSTANDING
W. S. MERWIN

Understanding Contemporary American Literature
Matthew J. Bruccoli, General Editor

Volumes on

Edward Albee • John Barth • Donald Barthelme • The Beats
The Black Mountain Poets • Robert Bly • Raymond Carver
Chicano Literature • Contemporary American Drama
Contemporary American Horror Fiction
Contemporary American Literary Theory
Contemporary American Science F iction • James Dickey
E. L. Doctorow • John Gardner • George Garrett • John Hawkes
Joseph Heller • John Irving • Randall Jarrell • William Kennedy
Ursula K. Le Guin • Denise Levertov • Bernard Malamud
Carson McCullers • W. S. Merwin • Arthur Miller
Toni Morrison's Fiction • Vladimir Nabokov • Joyce Carol Oates
Tim O'Brien • Flannery O'Connor • Cynthia Ozick
Walker Percy • Katherine Anne Porter • Reynolds Price
Thomas Pynchon • Theodore Roethke • Philip Roth
Hubert Selby, Jr. • Mary Lee Settle • Isaac Bashevis Singer
Gary Snyder • William Stafford • Anne Tyler
Kurt Vonnegut • Tennessee Williams

Published in Columbia, South Carolina, by the
University of South Carolina Press

Manufactured in the United States of America

01 00 99 98 97   5 4 3 2 1

Library of Congress Cataloging-in-Publication Data

Hix, H. L.
   Understanding W. S. Merwin / H. L. Hix
      p. cm.— (Understanding contemporary American Literature)
      Includes bibliographical references and index.
      ISBN 1–57003–154–1
      1. Merwin, W. S. (William Stanley), 1927– —Criticism and
   interpretation. I. Title. II. Series
   PS3563.E75Z69 1997
   811'. 54—dc21   96–51241

UNDERSTANDING
W. S.
MERWIN

H. L. HIX

UNIVERSITY OF SOUTH CAROLINA PRESS

CONTENTS

Editor's Preface   vii

Preface   viii

Acknowledgments   ix

List of Abbreviations   x

Introduction   Merwin's Career   1

Chapter 1   Guides   5

Chapter 2   Myth   23

Chapter 3   Apocalypse   43

Chapter 4   Ecology   60

Chapter 5   Society   74

Chapter 6   Love   90

Chapter 7   Family   105

Chapter 8   Hawaii   124

Chapter 9   France   140

Notes   158

Bibliography   174

Index   183

EDITOR'S PREFACE

The volumes of *Understanding Contemporary American Literature* have been planned as guides or companions for students as well as good nonacademic readers. The editor and publisher perceive a need for these volumes because much of the influential contemporary literature makes special demands. Uninitiated readers encounter difficulty in approaching works that depart from the traditional forms and techniques of prose and poetry. Literature relies on conventions, but the conventions keep evolving; new writers form their own conventions—which in time may become familiar. Put simply, *UCAL* provides instruction in how to read certain contemporary writers—identifying and explicating their material, themes, use of language, point of view, structures, symbolism, and responses to experience.

The word *understanding* in the titles was deliberately chosen. Many willing readers lack an adequate understanding of how contemporary literature works; that is, what the author is attempting to express and the means by which it is conveyed. Although the criticism and analysis in the series have been aimed at a level of general accessibility, these introductory volumes are meant to be applied in conjunction with the works they cover. They do not provide a substitute for the works and authors they introduce, but rather prepare the reader for more profitable literary experiences.

M. J. B.

PREFACE

I have written this book, in defiance of Wittgenstein's daunting maxim that "any interpretation still hangs in the air along with what it interprets, and cannot give it any support," because I have been intrigued for years by Merwin's poetry, and because I have been haunted by Joseph Brodsky's dictum that "every individual ought to know at least one poet from cover to cover: if not as a guide through the world, then as a yardstick for the language." I hope for this book only that my own attempt to fulfill Brodsky's imperative will help others to do so.

I am grateful to many people and institutions for their help with this book. William V. Davis introduced me to contemporary poetry and to the work of W. S. Merwin. Loren Graham gave me insights into particular poems years before I had even thought of this book. The students in my 1995 class on Merwin and Glück reminded me always to approach the poems with fresh eyes. The Kansas City Art Institute awarded me a semester's sabbatical leave, during which this book was written. Nancy Romero, Bruce Swann, and Kelly Bridgewater, archivists at the University of Illinois, were extraordinarily helpful during my research at the Merwin archive. My visits to Harvard University's Poetry Room were made productive by the help of Joyce Wilson and the ongoing support of its curator, Stratis Haviaras. Finally, I am indebted to my colleague Rush Rankin for his attempt, through painstaking criticism of an earlier draft, to "amend what flaws may lurk."

ACKNOWLEDGMENTS

Quotations from the following sources are reprinted by permission of Georges Borchardt, Inc.

A Mask for Janus. Copyright ©1952 by Yale University Press

The Dancing Bears. Copyright ©1954 by Yale University Press.

Green With Beasts. Copyright ©1955, 1956 by W. S. Merwin.

The Drunk in the Furnace. Copyright ©1956, 1957, 1958, 1959, 1960 by W. S. Merwin.

The Moving Target. Copyright ©1960, 1961, 1962, 1963 by W. S. Merwin.

The Lice. Copyright ©1963, 1964, 1965, 1966, 1967 by W. S. Merwin.

The Carrier of Ladders. Copyright ©1967, 1968, 1969, 1970 by W. S. Merwin.

Writings to an Unfinished Accompaniment. Copyright ©1969, 1970, 1971, 1972, 1973 by W. S. Merwin.

The Compass Flower. Copyright ©1977 by W. S. Merwin.

Finding the Islands. Copyright ©1982 by W. S. Merwin.

Opening the Hand. Copyright ©1983 by W. S. Merwin.

Quotations from the following sources are reprinted by permission of Alfred A. Knopf, Inc.

The Rain in the Trees. Copyright ©1988 by W. S. Merwin.

Travels. Copyright ©1993 by W. S. Merwin.

The Vixen. Copyright ©1995 by W. S. Merwin.

ABBREVIATIONS

CF	*The Compass Flower* (1977)
CL	*The Carrier of Ladders* (1970)
FF	*The First Four Books of Poems* (1975)
FI	*Finding the Islands* (1982)
L	*The Lice* (1967)
LU	*The Lost Upland* (1992)
MPC	*The Miner's Pale Children* (1970)
MT	*The Moving Target* (1963)
OH	*Opening the Hand* (1983)
RM	*Regions of Memory: Uncollected Prose, 1949–82* (1987) (ed. Ed Folsom and Cary Nelson)
RT	*The Rain in the Trees* (1988)
T	*Travels* (1993)
UO	*Unframed Originals* (1982)
WUA	*Writings to an Unfinished Accompaniment* (1973)
V	*The Vixen* (1996)

UNDERSTANDING
W. S. MERWIN

Merwin's Career

Many notable writers, from the European philosophers Kant, Kierkegaard, and Nietzsche to the American poets Cummings and Eliot, grew up in devout religious households. William Stanley Merwin, whose father was a "strict, unemotional" Presbyterian minister, belongs in that company.[1] Characteristics of the household in which he was raised, notably guardedness and a sense of moral urgency, pervade Merwin's work and help create his distinctive voice. These features make his poetry distinct in an age that prizes histrionic self-revelation in its poetry no less than its television talk shows and that sees art as something done either for its own sake or for no purpose at all.

W. S. Merwin was born on 30 September 1927 to William and Ann Merwin and lived in Union City, New Jersey, until his family moved to Scranton, Pennsylvania, in the mid 1930s. Even in a strict household with no special fondness for poetry, Merwin showed an early propensity for verse, composing hymns in childhood.[2]

Writing poetry did not become his passion, though, until his college years at Princeton. He was not a good student, spending by his own account more time riding horses at the university stable than in class (RM, 301), but he did earn a bachelor's degree in English in 1947 and then studied for a year in the Department of Modern Languages toward a master's degree he never completed. During that year he married Dorothy Jeanne Ferry, the secretary to a Princeton physicist.[3]

More important than his classes were the mentors he found at Princeton, notably poet/critic R. P. Blackmur and poet John Berryman. Years later, Merwin tried to articulate the influence of each. In a prose memoir, he said of Blackmur that "Richard was speaking for alternatives. To be discovered, invented, made. He was insisting that the artist—and by extension, the individual life—can have no formula for survival" (RM, 194). Blackmur possessed, and instilled in Merwin, "a tenacious esteem not for the human alone but for the inchoate in humanity, as it struggles inexplicably to complete itself through language" (RM, 199). Merwin credits Berryman with exuding a passion for poetry. Merwin reports in a poem that Berryman advised him to pray to the Muse and to paper his wall with rejection slips, and told him (fervently) that "the great presence / that permitted everything and transmuted it / in poetry was passion" (OH, 65).

After college, Merwin was a tutor in the household of Princess de Braganza of Portugal.[4] In 1950 and 1951, he lived on the Mediterranean island of Majorca, where he tutored the son of British poet Robert Graves. From Majorca, Merwin moved to London, where he supported himself by translating French and Spanish literature for the BBC Third Programme. In London, he met Dido Milroy, with whom he collaborated on a play called *The Darkling Child,* and who eventually became his second wife.[5]

The selection by W. H. Auden of Merwin's first book, *A Mask for Janus,* for the Yale Series of Younger Poets Award and its subsequent publication by Yale University Press in 1952 begins the long list of publications, prizes, and grants Merwin has received. His second book, *The Dancing Bears,* received a *Kenyon Review* fellowship. Even in drama, a genre Merwin abandoned early in his career, he received several fellowships, including a Rockefeller playwriting fellowship.

He worked for *The Nation* in the early 1960s, writing articles and serving briefly in 1962 as its poetry editor. During that time, having become increasingly disillusioned with an economy he saw as rapacious and with military policies he considered unduly belligerent, Merwin involved himself in the nascent resistance movement, and his poetry underwent a dramatic change from the traditional, formal poetry of the first four books to the stark free verse of the second four. This change in his poetry made its abrupt appearance in *The Moving Target,* published in 1963, not long after a decisive change in Merwin's personal life:

> Living in downtown Manhattan, the reverberations of the Cuban missile crisis seemed to become part of the ne-glected architecture itself. On the street corners and in the bars I heard the usual louts and loud-mouths declaring that "we should have dropped the bomb on [the Soviets] long ago." . . . I began to be pursued by the thought that if, in all this madhouse, someone were to ask me what I thought would be a good way to live, I would not have a very clear answer, and it seemed to me that it was time to try to find one.[6]

In 1954, he had used the inheritance left him by "Aunt Margie," his mother's cousin, to buy a farmhouse at Lacan de Loubressac, near Bretenoux, in southern France, and that farm became his refuge. "I realized that I did not know how to grow a single thing that I ate every day, and I decided to go back there and try to learn to grow food in the garden—something which all my peasant neighbors knew how to do."[7]

The themes and formal structures introduced in *The Moving Target* culminated in *The Lice* (1967) and *The Carrier of Ladders* (1970), still Merwin's most widely discussed books. For the latter, Merwin was awarded the Pulitzer Prize in 1971, but in a gesture that both his longtime editor Harry Ford (privately) and his first mentor W. H. Auden (publicly) declared ill-advised, Merwin took the award only as an occasion to protest "years of the news from Southeast Asia" and to express "openly a shame which many Americans feel, day after day, hopelessly and in silence" (RM, 272).

Separated by this time and soon to be divorced from Dido Milroy, having lived for some time in New York, Mexico, and France with his friend Moira Hodgson, and "looking to chart a new course," Merwin moved to Hawaii in the late 1970s, living at first with Dana Naone, "a Hawaiian and an aspiring poet" who shared Merwin's interest in Buddhism.[8] His relationship with Naone eventually ended, and in 1983 he married Paula Schwartz. Merwin has continued to live in Hawaii, where he is active in attempts to preserve Hawaiian culture and to restore the native flora and fauna.

W. S. Merwin is a Chancellor of the Academy of American Poets and a member of the American Academy of Arts and Letters. His many awards include the Bollingen Prize, the Fellowship of the Academy of American Poets, the Tanning Prize, the Lenore Marshall Prize, and the Lila Wallace-*Reader's Digest* Fellowship.

CHAPTER ONE

Guides

Poets seldom resist the temptation to comment, in one form or another, on poetry and especially on their own poems. Homer incorporated into his poems admonitions to treat poets with respect; Horace wrote entire poems on the subject of how to write poetry; Edgar Allan Poe wrote an essay explaining "The Raven"; the modern German poet Rainer Maria Rilke wrote a series of letters to a younger poet giving him advice about writing poetry; and so on. More recently, Robert Bly interspersed short explanatory essays in his *Selected Poems;* Donald Hall criticized contemporary poets for lack of originality, accusing them of writing the "McPoem"; Louise Glück connected the composition of her poem "Night Song" to the fire that had recently destroyed her house; and so on.

W. S. Merwin is no exception, commenting on poetry, and on his own poetry, frequently. Since his work has acquired a reputation for difficulty and obscurity, these comments function as guides and offer a good starting point for the project of understanding W. S. Merwin.[1] Two forms of that commentary are particularly valuable to readers of Merwin's work. One form is the essay, and the other is a type of poem called the *ars poetica.*

Even though Merwin's work has varied widely in theme and in style, the ideas about poetry formulated in his essays are broad enough to constitute an overview, so their advice about reading his work can apply to most of it. So far the only essays Merwin himself has collected into book form are the "reminiscences" in

Unframed Originals. Fortunately for his readers, Ed Folsom and Cary Nelson have included in *Regions of Memory,* a volume of Merwin's previously uncollected prose, some valuable essays, along with a substantial interview.

Merwin's richest poetic manifesto, called "On Open Form" (RM, 298–300), reveals many insights into his ambitions for his poetry, notably his preoccupation with time (especially with his own time), his desire to achieve an "unduplicatable resonance" rather than a recurring pattern, his wish that a poem be a form of testimony, and his belief that a poem's form and its content should be inseparable.

"On Open Form" is Merwin's contribution to an ongoing debate among poets and poetry readers about the relative merits of metrical verse vs. free verse. One point of view is typified by Robert Frost's statement that free verse resembles playing tennis with no net; the opposing point of view, by Robert Creeley's exclamation, "No wonder they insisted on those *forms!* They wouldn't know it *was* a woman unless she was wearing a dress."[2] Merwin's opening claim, that "what is called its form may be simply that part of the poem that had directly to do with time" (RM, 298), prepares him to reframe the terms of the dispute and to offer an alternative to the two standard views.

In the opening section of "On Open Form," Merwin says that those debating over whether metrical verse or free verse is better for making poems are asking the wrong question: the real issue is whether the form rightly relates the poem to its time.[3] In past ages, Merwin says, poets could be confident of "the role of time in the poem and the role of the poem in time," but contemporary poets, "for whom everything is in question," can "be sure of neither." Although poets in the Middle Ages could be confident of the form of poems, contemporary poets cannot.

The form of the poem rightly relates it to time only if the form is "a means, and is not made into an idol and loved for itself" (RM, 299). In the present time it must be a means for discovering "the patterns of a world of artifice" (RM, 298). The poets of the Middle Ages needed form to separate the poem from the world; poets today, according to Merwin, need form to help the poem find the world. Any form, whether metrical or free, that does not function as a means to this end is "mere confection." The form of the poem is a means of revelation about the world.

Merwin reveals another of his ambitions for his poetry when he says that in order for a "particular nebulous unwritten hope" to become a poem, it must achieve "an unduplicatable resonance, something that would be like an echo except that it is repeating no sound" (RM, 299). A poem, whether in metrical or free verse, may have a "manipulable, more or less predictably recurring pattern," but the *pattern* is not the *form.* The form is "something that always belonged to it: its sense and its conformation before it entered words." The unduplicatable resonance Merwin seeks is not only the con*for*mation, but also the con*fir*mation, of the poem. A duplicatable poem is not a poem at all. In prose, it may be possible to say something in more than one way, but not in poetry.

"On Open Form" also states a third ambition, Merwin's desire that the form of his poems be a testimony. Poetic form "is testimony of a way of hearing how life happens in time." Merwin wants a poetry of witness: specifically, witness to active, individual perception (a way of hearing) and to the development of an individual (how life happens in time). Merwin denies that either the words or time causes the form of the poem and gives a simple answer to what does: the poem causes its own form. "The visitation that is going to be a poem finds the form it needs" (RM, 300). A poem becomes a sonnet because it has to.

That answer to what causes the form of the poem is itself a fourth ambition, namely that form and content be one. "Obviously it is the poem that is or is not the only possible justification for any form" (RM, 300). A poem has failed if its content does not answer the question "Why that form?"; asked why a particular poem is a sonnet rather than a rondeau, the poet's only answer, Merwin implies, would be: Read the poem.

These ambitions combine to form an aesthetic of discovery. In a poem that realizes Merwin's stated ambitions, the act of reading will be like learning to hear something you have not heard before. The character Meno, in the Platonic dialogue that bears his name, asks Socrates, "How will you look for something when you don't in the least know what it is? How on earth are you going to set up something you don't know as the object of your search? To put it another way, even if you come right up against it, how will you know that what you have found is the thing you didn't know?"[4] Socrates answers Meno's question with the doctrine of recollection: you *did* know what you were looking for. Merwin answers with open form: the poem teaches you to hear what you have not heard before, and you know it when you hear it because the form and content of the poem are one.[5]

"On Open Form" reveals the degree to which Merwin's poetry is infused with ethical ideals. Merwin is a moral poet. This does not mean that he is "a man of blameless and upright life,"[6] nor that he is a didactic poet exhorting us to build "more stately mansions, O my soul, / As the swift seasons roll"[7]; only that his poetry is permeated by moral concerns.

In fact, each of the poetic ideals Merwin expresses in "On Open Form" replicates some well-known moral ideal. Merwin formulates the poem's relation to time in terms of an appropriate ordering of means and ends: the form must be a means to the poem, and the poem must be a means of discovery. Similarly, the German philosopher Immanuel Kant formulates the human agent's relation to duty in terms of an appropriate ordering of means and ends: one ought to treat other persons "always at the same time as an end and never simply as a means."[8]

Merwin's second ideal, the attainment of an unduplicatable resonance, so that the form exceeds mere pattern, has a correlative in Friedrich Nietzsche's praise of the hero who is more than the law, whose life creates a form rather than following the mere pattern of law. If for Merwin the form must be the poem's own expression, and any other kind of form is mere confection, for Nietzsche "a virtue must be our *own* invention, *our* most necessary self-expression and self-defense: any other kind of virtue is merely a danger."[9]

Merwin's third ideal, that a poem be a form of testimony, finds its analogue in the moral imperative, given in many religions, to "bear witness." To hoard truth for oneself when all humans wish for truth would be blameworthy, so religions that purport to possess truth instruct their practitioners to "Go forth to every part of the world, and proclaim the Good News to the whole creation."[10] Even outside of religion, the truth imposes obligation on those who gain access to it: in Plato's allegory, those who have emerged from the cave into the light of the sun have an obligation to return, in spite of their reluctance, to those still bound in darkness.[11] In religion and philosophy, a visitation transforms the visited into a messenger; Merwin thinks the same is true of "the visitation that is going to be a poem."

Finally, his ideal of the inseparability of form and content has an analogue in the ethical ideal of integrity. Any manual on early childhood education, from Rousseau's *Émile* to Dr. Spock's popular guides, will advise its readers that children follow parents' and teachers' examples rather than their words. The expectation that becomes our moral imperative to "practice what you preach" is innate, and Merwin expects of poems just such an identity between what is said (form) and what is done (content).

"On Open Form" is a useful guide to understanding Merwin's poetry, but there are also guides within the poetry itself. The term *ars poetica,* Latin for "the art of poetry," refers to poems that give advice about poetry or advocate a particular view of poetry's nature or function. Although Merwin seldom explicitly identifies a poem as an *ars poetica,* many of his poems read as such. Because they recur throughout his books, these poems about poetry help to show how Merwin's ideals and purposes have developed, and therefore give better clues than do his essays about the particular aspirations that shape individual books. Looking at one *ars poetica* from each of his books of poetry reveals in outline the overall pattern of Merwin's development that the following chapters will trace in more detail.

In the first four books, the poems about poetry establish some of the aims that will be constant throughout Merwin's career. The first such poem, "For a Dissolving Music," the seventh poem in his first book, introduces a theme that will persist through all of Merwin's poetry: recognition of the power wielded by what is unseen or immaterial or absent. Of the objects that answer the five questions posed in the poem, the defining feature is in each case precisely what is *not* present. To the question "What shall be seen?" the answer, "Limbs of a man," is qualified by absence: the limbs that will be seen belong to someone not there, because he is "going and gone." The "rime" that will be heard is hollow, and each of the items to be known is similarly qualified: a "blown and broken" house will not shelter a family, a draughty room does not shut out the cold, and a dry honeycomb nourishes neither bees nor humans.

To his own question "What shall be said?" the speaker begins with the qualification that perhaps nothing at all will be said. If something *is* said, the news is not good: time, the measure of human life, and blood, its source, "are spent money, / rain in a sieve."[12] The litany describing what might be said ends with a couplet, "shaken sleeve / empty of love," that portends one of the most famous images from the later poetry, in which Merwin makes vivid the ability of what is not there to have momentous consequences for what is: "my words are the garment of what I shall never be / Like the tucked sleeve of a one-armed boy" (L, 62). Similarly, absence permeates the list of what shall be sung, from the inability to support movement suffered by joints with spavin to the lack of necessary warmth in chill-driven blood to the nonexistent hope for heaven.

The Dancing Bears includes an *ars poetica* specifically identified as such. Whether or not its speaker stands for Merwin himself, "On the Subject of Poetry" does draw attention to at least two features that persist through all of Merwin's work. First, poetry for Merwin is not hortatory. It does not set out to teach what it knows to the untutored reader, but to engage in the act of exploration that follows the admission with which this poem begins: "I do not understand the world, father." But poetry does not for that reason sink into empty aestheticism or art for art's sake. Poets need not choose between a didacticism like that of Alexander Pope, for instance, or idle self-reflexive poetry like that of Oscar Wilde. Indeed, the speaker in this poem, having already stated that he cannot be didactic (since he himself lacks understanding), states also that he cannot merely write poetry about poetry: "When I speak, father, it is the world / That I must mention" (FF, 100). And it is the world that Merwin will mention in his writing throughout his career, no matter how the particular themes change: from ecology in *The Lice* (1967) to love in *The Compass Flower* (1977) to family in *Opening the Hand* (1983).

"On the Subject of Poetry" also reveals the importance that the sense of hearing has for Merwin. The man slouching at the end of the garden is not *watching* "the wheel revolving in the stream," but *listening* to it. So intent is his listening that "He does not move / His feet nor so much as raise his head / For fear he should disturb the sound he hears." He even prepares himself for listening by listening. The visual image has been central to nearly all twentieth-century poetry, engendering poetic movements like "imagism" and the "deep image" school, and certainly Merwin looks in his poems for arresting images. But he also listens in his poems for sounds, from the "dawn-song" of "Fresh wind in high grass, cricket on plowshare, / Whisper of stream in the green-shadowed place" he hears in *A Mask for Janus* (FF, 42) to the sheep he hears "running on the path of broken limestone" in *The Rain in the Trees* (1988), their "coughing their calling and wheezing even the warm / greased wool rubbing on the worn walls" (32).

Green with Beasts opens with a dedicatory poem that is also an *ars poetica*. "To Dido" introduces a theme that will run through all of Merwin's work: the inadequacy of poetry, its inevitable failure. "Its mumbled inadequacy reminds us always / In this world how little can be communicated" (FF, 126). The lines of a poem signify—or try to signify—precisely that which cannot be expressed in words. They "are only tokens / Of what there is no word for," and they assert a power that exceeds the poet's control. "They themselves determine whose they are, / Announcing unbidden their conception / In a still place of perpetual surprise." By regarding what cannot be said as more important than what can be said, "To Dido" hints at one reason why silence becomes so central a theme in later poems like "A Scale in May" (L, 50) and "Words from a Totem Animal" (CL, 15).

The *ars poetica* poems in these early books identify a set of concerns—to speak about the world by referring to what is absent, in a medium that inevitably fails—that add up to a preoccupation with myth, the mode of communication in which those apparently conflicting concerns can coexist. "For every myth told, there is another, unnameable, that is not told, another which beckons from the shadows, surfacing only through allusions, fragments, coincidences."[13] Because myth allows the world to speak from the shadows, it establishes itself early in Merwin's career as his favorite way of thinking and writing.

After calling *Green with Beasts* Merwin's Genesis, Cheri Davis aptly calls *The Drunk in the Furnace* "his Job, celebrating the awesome power of the sea and of the unknown."[14] But his Job is also his Isaiah, prophesying the poet who is to come. Like the rest of the book, "Fog-Horn" (FF, 203) gives a premonition of what soon will flow from Merwin's pen. He will, with his next several books of poems (and his first two books of prose) imitate the fog-horn that "does not call to anything human / But to something men had forgotten." He will speak, like the fog-horn, not "in the light of clear day," but "when the shifting blindness" of war and large-scale ecological destruction "Descends and is acknowledged among us." Merwin's mature poems may, like the fog-horn, insist on something he never meant, but he will put them there, as "we" put the fog-horn there,

> To give warning of something we dare not
> Ignore, lest we should come upon it
> Too suddenly, recognize it too late,
> As our cries were swallowed up and all hands lost.

By the time of *The Moving Target,* Merwin's poems about poetry begin to reflect the drastic changes in his personal life and in his poetic ambitions. "Having come to feel dissatisfied with a way of writing, you don't simply say, 'I'm going to give up A, because I would prefer B.' At the point when you're making this decision, B doesn't exist, or at least you don't know what B is. So in a sense, you simply say 'I have to stop writing this way, it's finished. . . . If I go on writing poems like this, I'm imitating something. These aren't really poems.'"[15] "Invocation" puts the poet in just such a position, setting out from A to find B. "Here I am once again with my dry mouth / At the fountain of thistles / Preparing to sing" (MT, 40). The poet sings not from inspiration, a fullness of joy or knowledge or insight that comes from outside. "Your life and your writing don't come, finally, from your knowledge."[16] Instead, the poet writes from obligation, an imperative that comes from inside. One sets out to find a song as one sets out on a journey, to produce beautiful songs from a dry mouth. But the fountain of thistles, rather than the singing, reveals the broader focus of the book. By the time of *The Moving Target,* Merwin had begun to see the future as a barren, desiccated place, so his myth becomes a myth of apocalypse. He sees himself as "Walking at night between the two deserts," past and future, "Singing" (MT, 50).

By the time of *The Lice,* Merwin had completed the formal change he began in *The Moving Target.* One aspect of that change is the absence of punctuation in the poems, which Merwin explains by saying that he "wanted a quality of transparency. Punctuation nails the poem down on the page; when you don't use it the poem becomes more a thing in itself, at once more transparent and more actual."[17] The quality of transparency he seeks is described in "The Cold Before the Moonrise," one of several poems in *The Lice* that can be read as an *ars poetica.* He explicitly repudiates the style of the first four books, saying, "It is too simple" to "say I was born far from home" (L, 46), as he has done in the first four books with his poems of Odyssean journeys. Now he seeks "a place where this is the language." The "this" refers to the cold before the moonrise, something that is itself as transparent as Merwin wants his poems to be (one sees signs of the cold, but not the cold itself) and that culminates in the perfect clarity Merwin wants his poems to produce (the beauty and brightness of a moonlit night). That he wants a natural phenomenon to be his language foregrounds the emphasis *The Lice* places on the natural world and draws attention to the ecological concerns central to that book.

The Carrier of Ladders continues the project initiated in *The Moving Target* and brought to fullness in *The Lice*. The formal aspects of the project, the change from traditional stanza forms to "open form" and the removal of punctuation, coincide with a political change, so human society becomes the natural focal point for the project's culminating book. Merwin wrote the poems for all three books in the politically troubled 1960s, and he wants to circumvent the principle that "Poetry makes nothing happen,"[18] even though he knows that in the end that principle cannot be circumvented. "The part of you," he says, "that writes poems hoping that it will make something happen, which is the part of you that's writing propaganda, is always there. Poetry isn't so pure that it's completely devoid of that. You wouldn't want it to be. Pure poetry is an antimacassar, isn't it? It's a decoration. You do want something to happen, even if it is only to get somebody to move something. When we wrote poems during the Vietnam war we wanted the poems to stop the war."[19] But poems do not stop wars, so poets must envision new possibilities, conceptual alternatives not provided by the world that makes wars. That idea animates "Memory of Spring" (CL, 115). That "the first composer / could hear only what he could write" makes his writing all the more necessary. No poem of Merwin's more succinctly embodies his desire that poetry and people reconfigure the world.

GUIDES

"Song of Man Chipping an Arrowhead," from *Writings to an Unfinished Accompaniment,* connects Merwin's propensity for silence, absence, and negation with the long tradition of art, by calling to mind Michelangelo's idea that a sculptor finds the sculpture that is already present in the marble by removing everything that is not the sculpture.[20] If the "little children," the chips of stone, are analogous to poems, then the poet is trying to create something that is not in the poems themselves. This poem forms a perfect contrast to "Memory of Spring." There, Merwin's attempt to solve the poet's paradoxical desire to end war begins with acceptance of the premise that poetry makes nothing happen. Here, though, he looks on the other side of the paradox: even if poetry makes nothing happen, it reveals the arrowhead that can make something happen, and what the arrowhead makes happen is precisely bloodshed.

The Compass Flower finds Merwin renewing himself again, if not to the same degree at least in the same manner as he had done in *The Moving Target.* This time, though, he moves toward directness and simplicity of style, and toward affirmation rather than negation. These new tendencies are reflected in "Crossing Place" (CF, 42). Read as an *ars poetica,* the poem reports that Merwin is no longer trying to sing in front of the fountain of thistles, or to be the first composer, inventing a new song out of nothing; instead, he is trying simply to bring back "the pitcher of water / from the falls" without spilling it. The poet is not *making* something, but providing it. And the point is not political action, but sustenance. Water cannot prevent war, but it enables humans to live, and by 1977 Merwin seems to be thinking of poetry as thus similar to water. In *The Compass Flower,* he finds in love the sustenance for which he searches.

The thematic centrality of love continues into his next collection of poems. Even though *Finding the Islands* (1982) contains no obvious candidate for an ars poetica, the "Foreword" to *Asian Figures,* his translation and compilation of Oriental proverbs, reveals in "To Dana with the Gift of a Calendar" an expression of the poetic ideals he pursues in *Finding the Islands.* Merwin writes that

> there is an affinity which everyone must have noticed between poetry—certain kinds and moments of it—on the one hand, and such succinct forms as the proverb, the aphorism, the riddle, on the other. . . . There are qualities that they obviously have in common: an urge to finality of utterance, for example, and to be irreducible [sic] and unchangeable. The urge to brevity is not perhaps as typical of poetry as we would sometimes wish, but the urge to be self-contained, to be whole, is perhaps another form of the same thing, or can be, and it is related to the irreversibility in the words that is a mark of poetry.[21]

"To Dana with the Gift of a Calendar" simultaneously attempts to be self-contained and expresses the poet's wish to be whole. It looks on the page very much like the "Asian Figures" to which Merwin refers in the passage just quoted: tiny three-line, aphoristic stanzas, each of which, although it is in a string of similar stanzas, might perfectly well be in a different string or might even stand alone (as do two other poems in the book, "Sound of Rapids of Laramie River in Late August" and "Road"). The poet wishes for an analogous wholeness. Like one of the divided bodies in

Aristophanes' tale of the origin of love in Plato's *Symposium,* the speaker wants to be united with his lover as the sole condition for his completion. Thus when Merwin writes "In the winter in the first month of every / year of my life I was / looking for you" (FI, 41) or "we are attacked / and we / are one" (FI, 42), the poem—like love itself—embodies the ideals referred to in the "Foreword": finality, irreducibility, unchangeableness, self-containment, wholeness, and irreversibility.

If the poems of Merwin's late youth were apocalyptic, believing that human greed and violence had taken away his (and the world's) future, the poems of Merwin's later life will lament the loss not of the future but of the past. By 1983, the year that "Talking" was published in *Opening the Hand,* the greater part of Merwin's life is behind him, and he talks less about what will happen and more about "what has already happened" (OH, 22). His lament is not that the future is dead, as in "For a Coming Extinction" (L, 68), but that "what I want to talk about is no longer there" (OH, 22). Now "Whatever I talk about is yesterday," and in fact "the only way I can see today / is as yesterday." This inevitable attention to yesterday becomes for Merwin a fascination with his family, and results not only in the family poems in *Opening the Hand* but also the prose recollections in *Unframed Originals.* The change from anticipation to recollection recorded in those two volumes brings with it a change in mood. As he and his poems age, they are able to do what his poetry of the 1960s could not do: "laugh with surprise at what disappeared."

"Witness," the clearest instance of an *ars poetica* in *The Rain in the Trees,* emphasizes the purposefulness of poetry. Here is the poem, in its entirety:

> I want to tell what the forests
> were like
>
> I will have to speak
> in a forgotten language[.]

The speaker has something particular to say, but no shared
language in which to say it.[22] The poet is still in the difficult
position, identified years before in "To Dido," of wanting to
express what there are no words for, but the emphasis here is on
the fact that the purpose remains even if failure is inevitable. The
poet still tries—and ought to try—to tell what the forests were
like, even though the language he needs has been forgotten. For
Merwin, the attempt to tell what the forests were like and the
attempt to recover the forgotten language are joined in his attempt
to identify himself with Hawaii, a place whose forests he sees as
tragically ravaged and whose native language he sees as heed-
lessly ignored.

Perhaps the best *ars poetica* in Merwin's corpus is "Cover
Note," the poem that opens *Travels*. In that poem, Merwin
expresses his ambition that his poetry will be a means for human
unity, revealing that the world we cling to, "we cling to *in
common*" (ix, my italics). He wants his poems to be the occasion
for attentiveness, since the light that makes our days "shimmer"
is from our world's burning. He has abandoned the dream of
immortality for himself or his poems, replacing it with the hope
that "what passes between / us now in a silence / on this side of
the flames" will be "*our* true meaning" (ix, my italics), not his

meaning alone. As in the early poem "On the Subject of Poetry," he wants his words to embody the world, "the last rustling of // paws in high grass the one / owl hunting along this / spared valley" (x), because those are "our uncaught / voices." The human unity he desires will be achieved between the poet and the reader if his words "seem / as though they had occurred / to you" and if you "take / them with you as your own" (x).

At the time of this writing, Merwin's latest book is *The Vixen* (1996). Its *ars poetica*, "Vixen" (V, 69), not only exemplifies that book's unifying interest in recalling the years he lived in rural France, but also reads like the summation of a career. In it the speaker addresses a vixen, but the list of appellations with which he begins might also name the various aspirations of Merwin's poetic corpus:

Comet of stillness princess of what is over
    high note held without trembling without voice without
        sound
aura of complete darkness keeper of the kept secrets
    of the destroyed stories the escaped dreams the sentences
never caught in words warden of where the river went
    touch of its surface sibyl of the extinguished
window onto the hidden place and the other time[.]

This poem is Merwin's testament: "when I have heard you the soles of my feet have made answer / when I have seen you I have waked and slipped from the calendars / from the creeds of difference and the contradictions / that were my life." Here

Merwin expresses the wish in which all the concerns of his poetry culminate: "before the garden is extinct and the woods are figures / guttering on a screen let my words find their own / places in the silence after the animals."

Even though this chapter has looked at only a few of Merwin's guides to his own work, it should help to explain the organization of the chapters that follow. Since Merwin's poetry is *about* things, rather than being merely self-reflexive, the chapters are organized thematically. Since his books display an unusual integrity—seeming to read as a single poem rather than a collection of individual poems—the chapters focus on particular books in which the theme is prominent, rather than trying to trace the theme through Merwin's entire corpus. And since Merwin "has made his career what the word means: a course, a passage out,"[23] since, in other words, his books change substantially in style and substance from the first to the most recent, the chapters will follow a roughly chronological arrangement, starting with early themes and early books and ending with later themes and later books.

CHAPTER TWO

Myth

From the first published commentary on Merwin's poetry, W. H. Auden's preface to *A Mask for Janus,* readers have noticed a mythic sensibility in Merwin. Auden distinguishes between poetry where "the overt subject of the poem is a specific experience undergone by the 'I' of the poem" and poetry where "the overt subject is universal and impersonal, frequently a myth."[1] He places *A Mask for Janus* in the second category, where with few exceptions Merwin's poems stayed, at least until *The Compass Flower.*

Myth is prominent enough in Merwin's poetry that other readers since Auden have made even stronger claims for its centrality to his poetics, claiming that Merwin's poetry "assimilates both the purpose and the method of mythic thought," that in Merwin's mature poetry "the poet assumes the role of mythmaker,"[2] and that "his conception of the poet as myth maker" is "his aesthetic premise for poetry itself."[3]

Merwin himself has confirmed the centrality of myth in his work, implying that not only his poetry, but *all* poetry, is mythic: "I think that any real use of language is mythic in some sense," he says. "Language is a myth. Language is the articulation of myth."[4] Even more expansively, he has said that life itself has the form of myth and is thus "the ultimate myth. Life is really only the way we conceptualize the world, the way we come to understand what we think we experience. That's what the myth is."[5]

Merwin's own statements do not clarify the role myth plays in his work. For one thing, his conception of myth has changed along with his poetry, as he himself recognizes when he states in a 1984 interview that "my notion of what myth means would be very different from what I thought it meant when I was in my early career."[6] For another thing, Merwin himself admits that "myth is pretty hard to isolate" and declares himself at a loss to define it.[7] Finally, when Merwin does make gestures toward definition, they are too inclusive to be useful. Myth, he says in one interview, "is everything that helps us make sense of the world."[8] A definition of God as the whole universe fails to distinguish God from the Devil, and a definition of myth as "everything that helps us make sense of the world" fails to distinguish mythic from non-mythic poetry.

Merwin's own statements only confirm myth as something "that I would always want to be present in whatever I wrote."[9] Understanding its role begins with distinguishing two different forms myth takes in Merwin's poetry. In some poems he creates new myths, and in others he adapts established myths to his own purposes. Both of those forms of mythic sensibility occur in *Green with Beasts.*

The first part, "Physiologus: Chapters for a Bestiary," exemplifies the creation of new myths, and signals an increase in intensity over the first two books as his new myths initiate a deepening identification with animals. "His poetry of mythic and mystical exploration becomes progressively more convincing, in visceral human terms, as he begins to feel his way into animal consciousness, or at least into the mysterious realm between human and natural which is the source of much genuine myth. As he moves deeper into the animal world, he prospects for new myths rather than revising old ones."[10]

It is possible to create a non-mythic bestiary, as Elizabeth Bishop does in her three-part poem "Rainy Season; Sub-Tropics."[11] Like Merwin's, Bishop's bestiary meditates on a series of animals, but unlike Merwin's, Bishop's emphasizes the compilation of minute observations. Bishop's bestiary records the details of her subjects and enumerates their particular features. Of her first beast, a giant toad, Bishop records its external appearance, noting that the mist condensed on its skin runs down its back and from the corners of its mouth; she records its movement, counting the number of times it hops; she observes the manner of its noise-making and identifies the location of its poison sacs. Of her second beast, a strayed crab, Bishop notes its various colors (wine-colored body, saffron-yellow claw), its behavior, and its environment, down to the "skittering waterbugs that smell like rotten apples" (140). Of her third beast, a giant snail, she observes the size of its body, the manner of its movement, its body temperature, and the "lovely opalescent ribbon" it leaves in its path (141).

Merwin's bestiary contrasts sharply with Bishop's. Rather than recording the details of his beasts, Merwin identifies the conditions of their possibility. By using particulars only as a means to get to universals, Merwin plays Plato to Bishop's Aristotle. Bishop wants to know exactly how things are; Merwin wants to know just what they mean.[12] "Leviathan" (FF, 127) exemplifies this mythic bent in Merwin's bestiary. Just as *The Iliad* gives not descriptions of Athena that would allow us to paint her portrait but rather descriptions that reveal the significance of her actions, so in "Leviathan" the description leads the reader to "see" the creature, but only in the sense of "I see what you mean," not of "I see the brown cow." The reader sees not the black, finned mammal swimming through the ocean but "the black sea-brute bulling through wave-wrack."

In any myth, description is meaning-charged, as when Homer gives the catalog of ships in *The Iliad* or Matthew and Luke give their divergent genealogies of Jesus: the point is to establish not the historical "facts" but our affinity with the people in question. So with Merwin's "Leviathan." Instead of giving a description of size whose primary intent is to serve visualization (leviathan is as long as a football field), Merwin gives a description of size that establishes the beast's danger to humans.

> The hulk of him is like hills heaving,
> Dark, yet as crags of drift-ice, crowns cracking in thunder,
> Like land's self by night black-looming, surf churning and
>   trailing
> Along his shores' rushing, shoal-water boding
> About the dark of his jaws; and who should moor at his edge
> And fare on afoot would find gates of no gardens,
> But the hill of dark underfoot diving,
> Closing overhead, the cold deep, and drowning.

The description of the whale watching sunrise over the ocean establishes its relation to us, this time emblematic not of the awefulness of creation but (anticipating a theme that will become prominent in Merwin's later books) of the harmony of animals with the rest of nature. "He makes no cry / Though that light is a breath" (FF, 128). Like humans, he can look before and after: "with one eye he watches / Dark of night sinking last, with one eye dayrise." But unlike humans, he does not try to impose his will on nature; instead "he waits for the world to begin."

"White Goat, White Ram" (FF, 135) not only makes the animals mythic but comments self-consciously on the very process of doing so. As he had done with the leviathan, Merwin uses the goat and the ram as points of reference for understanding ourselves. That they have neither language nor memory marks their difference from humans. The goat is blind because she "has no names to see with: over her shoulder / She sees not summer, not the idea of summer, / But green meanings, shadows, the gold light of now." What she sees has all been "known before, / Perceived many times before, yet not / Remembered." But the poem shows that we attribute to those differences more importance than they possess. We seize on the animals' lack of language and memory, and "for our uses call that innocence," so that, as in the Abraham and Isaac myth, "when our supreme gesture / Of propitiation has obediently been raised / It may be the thicket-snared ram that dies instead of the son" (FF, 136). But as the goat and ram are to humans, so are humans to the angels, the speaker says. Humans too stand in a mystery, "for a mystery / Is that for which we have not yet received / Or made the name, the terms, that may enclose / And call it" (FF, 137). Human language and memory, too, are insufficient, so what appears at first to be a difference between humans and the beasts proves in the end to be a similarity.

Anthony Libby says that throughout *Green with Beasts,* Merwin "suggests that the silent mystery of animals, so often described as 'angels,' is either analogous to or the same as the ultimate and unnameable mystery of humans,"[13] and certainly he suggests that in "White Goat, White Ram." The mystery humans see and try to name in animals matches the mystery we do not see and cannot name in ourselves, but can only infer by extrapolating from the imagined experience of creatures whose vision is of a different order from our own. As is the case with the goat and ram, there is a road nearby that "we do not see as a road," not made by either "my preference or kind."

> Oh we cannot know and we are not
> What we signify, but in what sign
> May we be innocent, for out of our dumbness
> We would speak for them, give speech to the mute tongues
> Of angels.

That in *Green with Beasts* Merwin so identifies himself with animals, and so closely ties humans to animals, both foreshadows his later ecological concerns and confirms the value most often attributed to his use of myth.

> In pursuing myth, Merwin removed himself from the narrower, more personal concerns of most of his fellow poets; and while they were trying to make poems that corresponded to the breath, the pulse, or the movements of the mind, Merwin was busy enlarging the temple. What he discovered was that myth, by its very nature, is narrative, and yet it offers the opportunity for lyricism. Opening outward, it also shines a light inward, revealing the self in

the cosmos rather than the cosmos in the self. This is the profound difference in Merwin's poetry, the element that sets him apart from a majority of the poets of the past forty years.[14]

Myth helps Merwin avoid the trap of self-absorption, in other words, and forces him to see himself in the whale and in the goat.

Merwin avoids self-absorption not only in his new myths but also in his adaptations of established myths. "The Annunciation" (FF, 147), for instance, in which Merwin borrows from the Gospel of Luke the narrative of the angel Gabriel's declaration to Mary that she will bear God's son, enforces release from self-absorption by depicting awe, a recognition of "the essential difference between the spiritual realm and our own," which the poem accomplishes by "demonstrating the futility of human powers which attempt willfully to bridge the barriers between" the two realms.[15] If in a poem like "White Goat, White Ram" myth "places" us by showing that we are no better and no more powerful than what is bestial, in "The Annunciation" myth teaches us that we are powerless in the presence of the spiritual.

In Luke's brief third-person account of the annunciation, Gabriel tells Mary she will bear a son who will be king over Israel forever. She asks how this is possible, since she is still a virgin, and he replies that "The Holy Spirit will come upon you, and the power of the Most High will overshadow you; and for that reason the holy child to be born will be called 'Son of God.'"[16] Mary assents, replying, "I am the Lord's servant; as you have spoken, so be it." Merwin's account of the annunciation alters the original by shifting from the neutral third person to the more intimately engaged first person: Mary herself, not the dispassionate Luke, tells the story. That adaptation in itself accords with a consistent development throughout *Green with Beasts.* The whole book "marks a distinct change in the poet's evolution. No longer is his poetry the cry of a forlorn and despairing outcast; no longer does he treat myth and fable with skeptical and detached irony."[17] Neither skeptical nor detached, this poem begins with fear: "It was not night, not even when the darkness came / That came blacker than any night, and more fearful, / Like a bell beating and I under its darkness dying / To the stun of the sound." Having begun in fear, it ends in grief: "I moved away because you must live / Forward, which is away from whatever / It was that you had, though you think when you have it / That it will stay with you forever" (152).

The defining feature of Merwin's poem, though, is not the fear and grief. Its most drastic adaptation of the older myth is an ambiguity between the annunciation and the immaculate conception. The poem's title indicates that its subject will be the annunciation, the event in which Gabriel tells Mary she will bear God's son, but the poem itself appears to focus not on the annunciation but on the immaculate conception, the event in which the Holy Spirit causes Mary to conceive a child. The ambiguity is important because it plays on a residual ambiguity from the earlier myth. In the Gospel of John, Jesus' birth is told in a very different way: "In the beginning was the Word, and the Word was with God, and the Word was God." By blurring the distinction between annunciation (a verbal event) and conception (the event in which the divine becomes human), Merwin makes the word God.

MYTH

Randall Stiffler describes Merwin's Mary as "quite plainly confused," but if so, she has good reason: the visitation of the angel and the visitation by the Holy Spirit, both extrahuman events, are difficult to distinguish from each other. Consider this part of her description:

> Then the darkness began: it brushed
> Just lightly first, like it might be the wing
> Of a bird, a soft bird, that flutters,
> As it comes down. It brushed the hem of the light
> And in my eyes, where I was nothing. But grew
> Clouding between my eyes and the light
> And rushing upon me, the way the shadow
> Of a cloud will rush over the sunned fields
> In a time of wind; and the black coming down
> In its greatness, between my eyes and the light,
> Was like wings growing, and the blackness
> Of their shadow growing as they came down
> Whirring and beating, cold and like thunder, until
> All the light was gone . . . (FF, 148–49)

Is this a description of Gabriel's visit or the Holy Ghost's? The reader is left with no way of knowing, because Mary, too, was left with no way of knowing, or at least with no way of remembering.

Mary cannot distinguish between the annunciation and the immaculate conception for a simple reason: neither her language nor her memory is strong enough. The failure of language begins even before the event: "it is not whirring / It is so still, but you are drawn out on it / Till you are as empty as the hushed hour, / And there is no word for it at all" (FF, 148). The failure of language continues through the event: "And in the silence / And in the fullness it came, it was there / Like it had not come but was there, whatever it was / That above all I cannot name" (FF, 150). And it continues after the event: "I knew I was not the same / And could not say how" (FF, 151). And in the end, her "memory" of the event is identical to her forgetting it.

> And yet it is there in me:
> As though if I could only remember
> The word, if I could make it with my breath
> It would be with me forever as it was
> Then in the beginning, when it was
> The end and the beginning, and the way
> They were one; and time and the things of falling
> Would not fall into emptiness but into
> The light, and the word tell the way of their falling
> Into the light forever, if I could remember
> And make the word with my breath. (FF, 153)

"The Annunciation," then, resembles "White Goat, White Ram" in that the comparison with angels reminds us of the frailness of our language and our memory, and therefore of our consanguinity with beasts. Stiffler says of Merwin's Mary that her memory cannot grasp nor her language reproduce the breadth, depth, and intensity that her experience of the body of God possessed.[18]

Merwin's two approaches to myth (the creation of new myths and the adaptation of established ones) are not as different as at first they might seem. When he adapts established myths, he alters them in unexpected ways or exploits some previously unnoticed dimension of them. When he creates new myths, they share basic features of established myths; indeed without such shared features they would not be mythic.

The possibility of having a mythic theme without being an adaptation of an established myth raises another important distinction. Myth is sometimes on the surface of Merwin's poems, at other times in the "deep structure" of the poem. Poems like "Proteus" (FF, 101), "The Judgment of Paris" (CL, 22), and "The Last One" (L, 10) wear myth on their sleeves, but a poem like "Home for Thanksgiving" uses the structure of the prodigal son myth without that myth's being necessarily visible at first reading. Similarly, "Native Trees" (RT, 6) borrows the structure of the myth of the fall without that myth's appearing on the poem's surface. This observation can be extended to whole groups of poems: for instance, apocalypse, the subject of the next chapter, is itself a mythic structure Merwin uses repeatedly.

In *Green with Beasts,* "The Prodigal Son" (FF, 142) names its myth and thus is able to leave much unsaid. The narrative scaffolding need not be added because it is already present as soon as it is named: the restless son has asked his father for his portion of the inheritance, the father has given it to him reluctantly, the boy has wasted his inherited wealth on dissipation, and soon he will return (humbler and wiser) to his father, who will receive him joyously into the household again, overcoming in the process the jealousy of the other brother.

Like "The Annunciation," though, "The Prodigal Son" uses the myth as a set of expectations to subvert. "The Annunciation," instead of the expected description of the annunciation, focuses at least as much on the immaculate conception. In "The Prodigal Son," the expected emphasis on the son is matched by an equal emphasis on the father. That emphasis asserts itself at the beginning of stanza II. Throughout stanza I, the images of filth and desiccation lead the reader to assume the poem adopts the point of view of the son in his degradation: "Except for the flies, except that there is not water / Enough for miles to make a mirror, the face / Of the afternoon might seem an empty lake." The speaker leads the reader to "the ruled shade of this white wall" where "there is nothing." But at the beginning of stanza II the poem reveals that its point of view is the father's. "And the silence off on the hills might be an echo / Of the silence here in the shadow of the white wall / Where the old man sits brooding upon distance / Upon emptiness" (FF, 143). The filth and desiccation are the father's environment, not the son's.

> The flies crawl
> Unnoticed over his face, through his drooping
> Beard, along his hands lying loose as his beard,
> Lying in his lap like drying leaves; and before him
> The smeared stalls of the beasts, the hens in the shade,
> The water-crane still at the well-head, the parched
> Fields that are his as far as the herdsmen
> Are emptiness in his vacant eyes. (FF, 143)

By thus establishing the emptiness of the father to complement the mythic emptiness of the son, Merwin creates a space for echoes "so numerous that the whole poem would have to be quoted to account for all of them. 'Distance' occurs sixteen times in the poem's five pages, 'emptiness' seventeen times, and there are continual references to silence, vacancy, nothingness, hollowness, illusions, and mirages."[19]

This abrupt change, from the assumption that the poem adopts the son's point of view to the realization that it adopts the father's, prepares the reader for the irony of the poem. In the traditional myth, the prodigal son learns from his mistake what his more cautious brother already knew, but in Merwin's version, he discovers what his brothers will never know. His brothers gain the whole world (or at least their inheritances) but lose their souls, while the prodigal son forfeits his inheritance to gain his soul. The prodigal son left with great expectations: "He went out / Looking for something his father had not given, / Delights abroad, some foreign ease, something / Vague but distant" (FF, 145). He "wasted / His substance in wild experiment and found / Emptiness only." He learned, in other words, a lesson advocated in a text known to the Gospel writers and Merwin alike, that "all is vanity."

But that is precisely what his brothers do not know.

> The other sons asleep
> With their wives in complacent dreams
> Wait in emptiness and do not know
> That it is emptiness, that they are waiting,
> That the flies are wrong and hover in nothing,
> That distance is dead . . . (FF, 146)

The prodigal son did not achieve what later will become Merwin's ideal, that of "Noah's Raven": "Why should I have returned? / My knowledge would not fit into theirs" (MT, 10). But he has achieved a paradoxical fullness: Socrates' wisdom consisted in knowing that he was ignorant, and the prodigal son's fullness comes from knowing that all is emptiness. By "hoping / For little, he takes the first step toward home." And it will *be* a home for him, now that he is no longer deluded, as it will never be for his brothers, who "Wait between a substance that is not theirs / And an illusion that is another's."

"The Eyes of the Drowned Watch Keels Going Over" (FF, 195) belongs to the other category from "The Prodigal Son": it neither gives obvious indicators of its mythic content nor makes use of any particular pre-existing myth, but it shares with other myths the structure of the underworld journey of the dead. Foremost in Merwin's mind would be "western" sources: the Christianity of his youth, which includes an underworld inhabited by some of the dead, and the Greek myths, in which death means transportation to an underworld ruled over by Hades, brother of Zeus and Poseidon, and guarded by the watchdog Cerberus. But this mythic structure occurs often: ancient Japanese myths included both submarine and subterranean abodes of the dead, "Yakuts seem to survive in a hell 'below,'" and in Mesoamerican myths the dead journey to a subterranean world.[20]

Like all myths of afterlife in the underworld, this poem is thematically preoccupied with time. In a taped conversation between Merwin and Richard Howard, while discussing "The Eyes of the Drowned," Howard quotes Blake's line "Eternity is in love with the productions of time"; Merwin replies, "That's what it's about. That's what the *book* is about, too."[21] Indeed, one might say that's what *all* of Merwin's books are about.

But "The Eyes of the Drowned" does not merely rehash an overdone mythic theme. It is important to the poem that the underworld in this case is under the sea, not under land. For one thing, it gives the poem some of its most mesmerizing images: "Where the light has no horizons we lie. / It dims into the depth not distance. It sways / Like hair, then we shift and turn over slightly." More importantly, though, the sea is charged with meaning in Merwin's poetry. "In his sea poems, the highlight of *Green with Beasts,* . . . the sea represents to the poet, first of all, power: the bursting, violent, archetypal, primeval force with which Melville was concerned."[22] Because of its immense power, "the sea serves to describe the double-edged reality Merwin wants to capture. The sea, as a life-providing element, has always bewitched men in its duplicity, for its treachery is as great as its good, and is as unexpected as it is unknowable."[23]

In this case, the sea possesses the power of final separation. The ships "go over us swinging / Jaggedly, laboring between our eyes / And the light," but we will never again be on the ships and we will never again see the light as those on the ships see it. The sea, like the river Lethe in Greek mythology, also transforms that external separation into the internal state of forgetting, leading Merwin in a later poem, "The Current," to refer to the sea as "the Lethe of the whales" (WUA, 24). The drowned cannot remember their lives or their deaths. They can see the ships "Churning their wrought courses / Between the sailing birds and the awed eyes / of the fish" and can ask why "the light shakes around them as they go," but they cannot answer their own question.

> Why? And why should we, rocking on shoal-pillow,
> With our eyes cling to them, and their wakes follow,
> Who follow nothing? If we could remember
> The stars in their clarity, we might understand now

> Why we pursued stars, to what end our eyes
> Fastened upon stars, how it was that we traced
> In their remote courses not their own fates but ours.

What is true of "The Eyes of the Drowned" is true of many of Merwin's poems: even in poems that do not "look" mythical, myth or at least the structure of myth is often at work.

The centrality of myth does not stop with Merwin's early poetry but extends into his mature work. In a 1987 article, in the course of explaining the dominant contemporary metaphors for how a poem works, Charles Molesworth identifies important features of myth in Merwin's mature verse. "To strip one's words of most particularity and specific detail, and still to write a highly charged syntax so that instead of vague emotive drift one creates a portentous but abstract narrative tension, to use a certain group of nouns like door, stone, ring, or feather that vaguely resemble the key objects in a primitive ritual: all of this comes together . . . to form a poetic language with a definite 'mythic' feel." Molesworth says, "There is often a vague 'other' in the poem, often a use of certain mythological topics, such as an etiological or apocalyptic terminus for the action, and often a stylized repetition or ambiguity to suggest ritual structure." Finally, Merwin's "poems are more like hierophantic testaments than songs."[24] Nowhere are the characteristics Molesworth describes more evident than in *Writings to an Unfinished Accompaniment,* not Merwin's best book but the one with the strongest "'mythic' feel."

The myth of the Odyssean journey underlies almost all the poems in *Writings.* The Odyssean journey myth has always been important to Merwin, and he had used it often before, but by the time of *Writings* it had assumed a new importance. The Vietnam War, the dominant political event for the United States during the writing of *The Lice* and *The Carrier of Ladders,* was nearing its end; in fact, the cease-fire agreement was signed in January 1973, the month in which *Writings* was published. This meant that thousands of veterans, and in an important sense the entire country, were in a position like that of Odysseus in *The Odyssey:* returning home from a decade-long war in a distant country, fought for what seemed to most of the combatants like someone else's cause.

Therein lies the importance of Victor Contoski's observation that "almost every poem in *Writings to an Unfinished Accompaniment* concerns travel," and typically "these journeys involve a search, usually a search for a meaningful life in a world apparently devoid of meaning."[25] The Odyssean journey is not merely a return home, but a return to meaning from a place without meaning: a place where people fight and die for reasons they do not understand or for causes they do not support.

Some of the Odyssean journeys in *Writings* echo Odyssean journeys that occur in earlier books. "Travelling" resembles the earlier "Odysseus" (from *The Drunk in the Furnace*) in its portrayal of the temporal isolation of the traveller:

> One travels
> to learn how not to look back
> hearing the doors fall down the stairs
> and the tongues like wet feathers in a high wind
>
> only in the present are the voices
> however far they travel. (WUA, 108)

One is trapped in the present no matter where one goes, as is Odysseus in the earlier poem. There, the traveller cannot maintain a consistent distinction between islands that are not home and islands that are, because "home" is in the past and the future, not in the present, and consequently cannot maintain its identity. Because one is trapped in the present wherever one goes,

> it was the same whether he stayed
> Or went. Therefore he went. And what wonder
> If sometimes he could not remember
> Which was the one who wished on his departure
> Perils that he could never sail through,
> And which, improbable, remote, and true,
> Was the one he kept sailing home to? (FF, 201)

That Merwin's Odysseus and Vietnam veterans endured the same difficulty returning home to meaning from meaninglessness, even though "Odysseus" was written before the war, reveals myth's ability to convey commonalities of experience. That "Travelling" so closely resembles the much earlier "Odysseus" demonstrates the flexibility and enduring power of mythic themes.

But Contoski points out a twist in *Writings:* "Not only people take journeys in Merwin's work; objects, even abstractions, join the search."[26] His example is "Bread" (WUA, 27), a poem in which "Each face in the street is a slice of bread / wandering on / searching," but there are numerous other examples. In "Habits" (WUA, 28), the speaker's habits fly "deeper into the century / carrying me." In "Mist" (WUA, 55), "the nuthatch blows his horn / leading a thin procession of white wind // past the black trees / through the world." And in "Under the Migrants" (WUA, 18), it is "flocks of single hands" that "are all flying / southward." In the earlier books, Merwin began identifying with animals. By the time of *Writings,* that identification has extended even to inanimate objects. We may travel alone, but we are not the only ones who must travel.

That we are trapped in the present makes the return to meaning from meaninglessness difficult, but Odysseus does return home, and so do many of the wanderers in Merwin's poems. In spite of the nihilism often attributed to these poems, there is a hope in them. "Like acts of magic, many of these visions compel belief as they resist explication; without apology they are based on the conviction that the miraculous is the ground of existence."[27] The miraculous is, in fact, the most effective way of restoring meaning to a meaningless world, and its inexplicable magic, according to David Baker, has given Merwin's work what power it has: "its attempt to negotiate between our failing world and another kind of experience—impersonal, dreamlike, symbolic. He tries to create a mythic, other world perhaps preferable to this one with its Vietnams and Watergates and pollution."[28]

Contoski arrives at two conclusions that help to connect the theme of this chapter, myth, with an assertion I made in the preceding chapter about Merwin's writing as a whole, namely that Merwin is a moral poet. The first conclusion recognizes that Merwin uses the Odyssean journey as a *moral* journey: "the philosophical basis" of the poems in *Writings* "finds its expression time and again in the metaphor of life as a moral journey."[29] The second conclusion explains *how* Merwin makes the journey into a moral journey. "These journeys, whether in space or time—often in both—lead to a remote period or place which affords a perspective on the present, a vantage point from which to make moral judgments on our lives."[30] That second conclusion also prepares for the next chapter: Merwin is preoccupied with apocalypse because it provides a foundation for a moral judgment of the present. He will watch with apprehension as "around me birds vanish into the air / shadows flow into the ground," but he will also believe that when "before me stones begin to go out like candles" they are "guiding me" (WUA, 106).

Merwin's use of myth—specifically Odyssean myth—continues. William Marling says of *The Compass Flower,* the book that follows *Writings,* that "his concern with the figure of Odysseus as a metaphor for modern unrest peeks out everywhere. Ships, ports, enchanted isles, and navigators provide subjects; land is, indeed, only a 'stone boat.'"[31] But viewing Merwin as, in Mark Christhilf's term, "the mythmaker" is to look at only one facet of a multifaceted body of work that demands to be considered from other angles as well.

CHAPTER THREE

Apocalypse

Even some of Merwin's best readers have been misled by myth's pervasiveness into treating it as the most fundamental element in his work, overlooking something even more basic. Although Merwin abandoned his early interest in the theater in favor of lyric poetry, myth functions for him in the same way it did for the fifth-century B.C. Athenian dramatists: as the vehicle for a tragic vision of the world. That tragic vision, rather than myth per se, defines the character of Merwin's work.

Merwin's tragic vision is that human individuals are implicated in and bear responsibility for some things not wholly in their power. If a human could be guilty only of something completely in her or his control, all stories would have a morally happy ending. That people sometimes have to "choose between the animal in the road / and the ditch,"[1] that even those who recycle newspapers and soda cans remain complicit in human destruction of the environment, makes stories tragic.[2]

The Moving Target is Merwin's first "mature" work, not for the reason usually cited (its use of open forms instead of the metrical verse patterns on which the first four books relied), but because in it his tragic vision receives its first full manifestation. By claiming Janus as his god in his first book, Merwin declared his intention to look simultaneously toward the past and toward the future, but in the first four books the face that sees the past dominates, choosing conventional forms and traditional subject matter. *The Moving Target* is written by Janus' other face.[3] The poems in his first four books assume the posture of sage; in *The Moving Target,* Merwin poses as prophet. He looks toward the future, and what he sees is the end. Because he is looking toward the future through a tragic lens, he is forced to abandon the faith in human progress common in America and typified by Walt Whitman. Unlike Whitman's melioristic poetry, Merwin's poetry becomes apocalyptic.

From the beginning of his career, the "alliance between myth and poetry" has given Merwin "perspective and scope which allows him to write pertinently about the contemporary world without succumbing to the fallacy of assuming that his problems are unique."[4] But the transition to open forms and the consequent focus on prophecy take him even farther from that fallacy. By applying his tragic vision to history, Merwin develops a premonition of impending catastrophe, a problem that if real is the problem of every human.

Intimations of the theme of apocalypse occur from the beginning of Merwin's work. For instance, in his first book he includes a poem that renovates the myth of the universal flood. "Dictum: For a Masque of Deluge" details elements of the stage setting and production for an imagined drama. The setting and production are simple: "Noah's ark is a basket, and the creatures entering are represented by the shadows they cast, while those excluded appear painted on a wheel above the stage."[5] The drama, though, is unmistakably apocalyptic: Noah is depicted preparing for the flood he knows is coming to destroy nearly all living things on earth. One man stands "by the ark, / Drunken with desolation" (FF, 39). His eyes "chase / A final clatter of doomed crows"; they "seek / An affirmation, a mercy, an island," but they "find only / Cities of cloud already crumbling."

In this early poem, though, Merwin has not yet attained the tragic vision that will characterize his mature poems. His portrayal of the end in this early work is derived from the work of others and backs down from finality. In "Dictum," Merwin "is following the lead of T. S. Eliot, Spengler, and other prophets of doom in predicting the imminent collapse of contemporary civilization, but he obviously does not believe in the finality of any such disaster: there is always a new birth, a new civilization, to replace the old."[6] The story ends not by identifying with the mass of humans and animals destroyed by the flood, but by embodying the point of view of Noah, who is granted

> the sigh of recession: the land
> Wells from the water; the beasts depart; the man
> Whose shocked speech must conjure a landscape
> As of some country where the dead years keep
> A circle of silence, a drying vista of ruin,
> Musters himself, rises, and stumbling after
> The dwindling beasts, under the all-colored
> Paper rainbow, whose arc he sees as promise,
> Moves in an amazement of resurrection,
> Solitary, impoverished, renewed. (FF, 40)

Merwin had not fully developed his own sense of apocalypse prior to *The Moving Target,* but he had been prepared by his childhood to begin the process of developing it. Not only did his father recount in sermons biblical prophecies concerning the end of the world, but other family members also would have shared the religiously based forebodings. He tells in *Unframed Originals* of a visit he made as an adult to his father's sister, Mary, who had lived in the same house with Merwin when he was a child and who had participated for some years in raising him. Merwin had visited her with the intention of inquiring about his ancestors, but she, by then old and even more hard of hearing than she had always been, kept drifting into religious talk. "There were not many more to go, now, and the last ones would not even die. They would live on, here, in the Kingdom of Heaven on Earth, for a thousand years, she insisted, and she told me to think about that. And at the end of that age, the world would end, and time and everything would be finished, and then the saved would be taken up into heaven; it was right there in scripture, and she could show it to me" (UO, 76). Whether or not Mary's particular preoccupations had the same shape in Merwin's childhood as they did at the time of this visit, it is clear that Merwin was surrounded in his childhood and youth by talk of The End, and specifically of the end as that which judges the present.

Even though his childhood had prepared him for a sense of impending catastrophe, that sense is not fully realized from the beginning of *The Moving Target,* but instead the poems record that development as they progress. All the narrator knows at the beginning is that "I must get a new flag, / I've buried enough under this one" (MT, 52). The first few poems are not so much visions of the world's future as they are declarations of independence from Merwin's past. "Home for Thanksgiving" is a departure poem whose conclusion resembles Frost's "I took the one less traveled by, / And that has made all the difference."[7] Satirical repetitions of "Well this is nice" decorate Merwin's description, because his own 'road not taken' *is* "nice" in the pejorative sense of that word. Out on a street car, away from the others,

I was thinking maybe—a thought
Which I have noticed many times like a bold rat—
I should have stayed making some of those good women
Happy, for a while at least, Vera with
The eau-de-cologne and the small fat dog named Joy,
Gladys with her earrings, cooking and watery arms, the one
With the limp and the fancy sheets[.] (MT, 3)

But he knows better than to enact that thought.

Two descriptions of himself as a ship, first as a "crusty / Unbarbered vessel launched with a bottle" (MT, 2) and then as "a ship in a bottle" (MT, 3), prepare for his evaluation of 'those good women': "They would have wanted to drink ship, sea, and all or / To break the bottle." Thus prepared, the evaluation of the women captures their ambiguity: they want both to break the bottle that launches him in order to authorize and thereby control his journeys, and to break the bottle that contains him in order to consume him. Threatened by two different forms of oblivion, he concludes that escaping the family is "the right thing after all."

Two other departure poems early in *The Moving Target* serve as transitions from Merwin's first four books, in which his mythic sensibility is the most prominent feature, to the full development of his tragic vision and an apocalyptic view of history. "Lemuel's Blessing" and "Noah's Raven" both appeal to traditional myths, as did so many of his earlier poems, but both move toward the identification with animals that becomes a frequently recurring feature of the second four books of poems.

The name Lemuel is derived from

the Old Testament King of the Hebrews mentioned briefly at the end of the Book of Proverbs. The reader may recall that King Lemuel's short speech (Proverbs XXXI: 1–31) repeats advice on how to be a good and righteous ruler which his mother has given him: "Give not thy strength unto women, nor thy ways to that which destroyeth kings"; avoid getting drunk; judge righteously when the poor and needy stand on trial before your throne; and find yourself a virtuous wife. In brief, Lemuel seems to be an archetype or model of all that is moral, just and prudent; and he guides people with law and order. Lemuel is, in effect, the symbol of the civilized community.[8]

In that sense, the poem is as tradition-laden as any from Merwin's first four books. Lemuel even "prays within a structure used by many of the great Psalms—in specific, the Lament Psalm."[9] Merwin's Lemuel, though, does not come straight from the Bible but has been filtered through the Lemuel of the poem's epigraph from Christopher Smart, and the Lemuel who emerges is no symbol of, but rather a longing to escape from, the civil community. Merwin's Lemuel holds a paradoxical position: "one who is an archetype of civilized tribal values petitions in a traditionally communal form of prayer that he be allowed to exist outside of civilized communal values, categories, definitions, approval and rewards, and come to share as deeply as possible the nature and characteristics of the wolf."[10] This paradoxical position is the preparation for what will develop by the end of *The Moving Target* into Merwin's apocalypticism. He had to recognize first civil society's destructive effects on himself in order to see its destructive effects on the environment (chapter 4) and its self-destructive effects (chapter 5). Distancing himself from civil society enables him to evaluate that society from an apocalyptic perspective.

One concern in this poetry, therefore, "as the title *The Moving Target* indicates, is with motion, and with the future in relation to the past."[11] The poet must move away from the past, and "Lemuel's Blessing" declares his intent to do so.

> Let my ignorance and my failings
> Remain far behind me like tracks made in a wet season,
> At the end of which I have vanished,
> So that those who track me for their own twisted ends
> May be rewarded only with ignorance and failings.
> But let me leave my cry stretched out behind me like a road
> On which I have followed you.
> And sustain me for my time in the desert
> On what is essential to me. (MT, 8)

Only by moving away from the past can the poet see the future clearly, only by seeing the future clearly can he rightly judge the present, and only by rightly judging the present can he accomplish what his apocalyptic vision aims for: the discovery of "what is essential."

The departure begun in "Home for Thanksgiving" and developed in "Lemuel's Blessing" is completed in "Noah's Raven" (MT, 10). Instead of merely selecting a totem animal and petitioning it as does Lemuel, the speaker in "Noah's Raven" *becomes* the bird. Lemuel knows he should depart, and his prayer is partly an attempt to gather the necessary courage, but the raven has already departed. He has made his home in "the desert of the unknown," because the known cannot accommodate him. Only the unknown is "big enough for my feet." The raven understands the necessity of apocalyptic vision: "the future splits the present with the echo of my voice."

There are continuities here with the earlier books: "the themes of *The Moving Target* are not new; they are merely disguised. Merwin's old preoccupation with the anabasis motif, with the classic voyage and the lonely journey on a dangerous road, persists, as does the theme of the return, of the prodigal son come home."[12] But these first poems in *The Moving Target,* if they do not constitute a new range of themes, do constitute a significant *development* of the established themes: the lonely wanderer and the prodigal son in the earlier books long for home, but the speakers in "Home for Thanksgiving," "Lemuel's Blessing," and "Noah's Raven" long to *escape* from home.

The thematic development is inseparable from the formal changes that begin in *The Moving Target.* Merwin's sense of apocalypse developed in part because he began to see the language itself as a warning. Our language, he says, is telling us "something about the quality of our own existence. It is telling us at the moment that the quality of our existence as a species, as a time, a moment in geologic and astronomic and historic time, is in great, great danger. It's in terrible jeopardy."[13] For a poet, such a recognition makes apocalypse "both an artistic and an ontological crisis"[14]: it demands that one change one's use of language along with one's attitude toward the world. Wittgenstein points out that "a confession has to be a part of your new life,"[15] but for the Merwin of *The Moving Target* the converse is also true: his living "differently for a number of years"[16] had to result in a new confession, a new way of using words.

Merwin's new way of using words included the highly visible change from traditional metrical stanza forms to open form, but it also entailed a new vocabulary. "*The Moving Target* reads like the grammar of a new dialect: its vocabulary, unlike Merwin's earlier far-flung raids on the *Oxford English Dictionary*, is severely limited. Certain nouns recur: bottle, shoe, knife, mirror, window, lock and key, door, hand, glove, feet, cup, ticket, dial. These concrete terms seem animate with a life of their own, a mysterious life which it is the poet's fate and mission to observe, express, interpret."[17] It is as if Merwin wants to create a periodic table of words whose various combinations will make his poems work like chemistry.

That animated vocabulary takes Merwin away from home, but not immediately into the full vision of apocalypse. After the departure poems at the beginning of the book comes a sequence of poems that depict the emptiness of a present divorced from the past. Connection between the past and the present provides both a sense of direction and a sense of continuity, but in "The Ships Are Made Ready in Silence" the narrator has lost direction and continuity alike. His compass is hooded like a falcon, so he does not know where he is going. His "memory of you" is fragmented into "broken bits which never left port" (MT, 23). He cannot choose, because any choice would contain "our destination / Circled with loss as with coral." He is confined to an isolated present that, since it has neither memory nor destination, neither past nor future, can hold no meaning.

> At this moment I could believe in no change,
> The mast perpetually
> Vacillating between the same constellations,
> The night never withdrawing its dark virtue
> From the harbor shaped as a heart,
> The sea pulsing as a heart.

Nothing is left him but emptiness.

Since that emptiness is in part the absence of a future, it will be interminable. "I have nothing new to ask of you, / Future, heaven of the poor," he says in "Another Year Come" (MT, 33). Isolated in the present moment, only empty repetition is possible. "I am still begging the same question / By the same light, / Eating the same stone." Even endless repetition, though, does not generate knowledge: "You would think we would know the present when it came," he says in "Now and Again" (MT, 31), "And would remember what we knew." But we do not. When "I try to remember what I almost heard" (MT, 41), the poet only hears "the locks close / And the lark take the keys / And hang them in heaven."

This second stage of *The Moving Target,* in which the isolation and futility of the present appears, culminates in "Second Sight" (MT, 42). The isolation from both past and future appears in the first stanza.

APOCALYPSE

> Turning the corner I
> Realize that I have read this before.
> It is summer. The sun
> Sits on the fire-escape while its children
> Tear their voices into little shreds.
> I wish I could remember how it ended.

Turning the corner does not get the narrator to the future as it should, and in fact the sun (whose movement provides a measure of the progress of time) is itself idle. But the narrator cannot reach the past, either, since memory fails him.

The narrator names capacities he thinks he should have, but doesn't: "I should know / The motive for the laundry," but he doesn't; "I should be able to call / Most of the windows / By their christian names," but he can't. These inabilities, combined with the isolation of the present from the past and the future, make even the present disorienting: "It's the old story. / Every morning something different is real" (MT, 43). His most powerful statement of present futility and meaninglessness occurs at the end of this poem:

> Here it is, the one and only,
> The beginning and the end.
> This time the dials have come with the hands and
> Suddenly I was never here before.
> Oh dust, oh dust, progress
> Is being made.

The turning point that ushers in his full vision of apocalypse occurs in "Vocations" (MT, 49). There Merwin makes the crucial connection between the emptiness of the present and the emptiness of the future: "Seeing how it goes / I see how it will be: / The color leaves but the light stays, / The light stays but we cannot grasp it." That connection enables him to find in the future an evaluative tool for the present: I can "wash my shadow in the river" because "The hands of the water have found tomorrow." The evaluation of the present by the future is the fundamental insight from which he will derive at least the rest of *The Moving Target* and *The Lice.*

His manner of articulating that insight in "The Crossroads of the World Etc." makes that poem a crossroads for Merwin's poetry. The last of the formal innovations in this book begins here: the question mark that ends this poem also abruptly ends Merwin's use of punctuation in his poetry. He will return to metrical stanza forms in *Travels,* late in his career, but not to punctuation.[18] More importantly, the sense of apocalypse that will drive his next books is complete. "I would never have thought I would be born here," the poem begins, stating the narrator's impulse to locate himself, but with a twist in the continuation: "So late in the stone so long before morning / Between the rivers learning of salt" (MT, 62). He wants to locate himself in time as well as space. He is late, yet far from a new beginning. And even his location in space is itself a location in time: rivers learn of salt when they empty into the sea, which is also when they end. The "rivers learning of salt" are in this poem only the first of many announcements of the end.

APOCALYPSE

Before me

The bird of the end with its
Colorless feet
Has walked on windows

I lose the track but I find it
Again again. (MT, 63)

Like a Greek god, the end is capable of assuming any form: first
rivers, now a bird.

Merwin's vision of apocalypse leads him to infer his own
responsibility to name the ruin: "Ruin / My city / Oh wreck of the
future out of which / The future rises / What is your name as we
fall." Apocalypse gives Merwin a way of addressing the paradox
of writing—an act whose usefulness is its preservation of ideas
or information for the future—in a time so near the end: his poems
can imitate Keats's name writ on water by becoming "clouds on
which I have written / Hope" (MT, 64). It anticipates his criticism
of technology in *The Lice* and *The Carrier of Ladders:* "The
trains on the / Trestles faster than their lights" outrun themselves.

The vision culminates in a metaphor, the empty garment,
that will become a staple of Merwin's poetry and a symbol for
him of irremediable spiritual emptiness.

Tomorrow,
The oldest man
Is throwing food into empty cages

Is it to me
He turns his cobweb
I go toward him extending
My shadow taking it to him
Is it to me he says no

Is it to me
He says no no I haven't time
Keep the lost garment, where would I find the owner? (MT, 66)

Merwin has discovered that tomorrow, even if it cannot fill out
the empty garment, at least *wants* to do so, and this insight will
sustain him through the poems that follow.

As the medieval Christian theologians felt compelled by
their intuitions of God to follow the via negativa, the belief that
God's nature so transcends human understanding that no positive
statements about it are accurate, so Merwin feels compelled by
his intuition of apocalypse to follow his own via negativa, which
he articulates in "For the Grave of Posterity" (MT, 71): "listen
you without vision you can still / hear it there is / nothing it is the
voice with the praises / that never changed that called to the
unsatisfied." The stone that marks the grave of posterity "is /
not here and bears no writing." Its message is already lost on us:
"whatever it could have said of you is already forgotten."

"For the Grave of Posterity" confirms the most important
observation about the sense of apocalypse Merwin develops in
The Moving Target and expands in *The Lice* and *The Carrier of
Ladders:* his apocalyptic vision is not a historical claim, not a
prediction of some future event, but rather a description of a

current state. "It transcends the conventional references to the Nazi holocaust and to nuclear war to refer more broadly to a sense in America that our origin and continuing presence as a people is apocalyptic. . . . Again and again, we rush forward to come into the emptiness of ourselves."[19] Merwin's apocalypse is not something soon to happen, but something happening now. The "essential existential problem posed by apocalypticism," William V. Davis says, is "that the end of time is actually to occur not only within time, as an end of time, but that it is to occur in *this* time."[20] The premise for Merwin's poems of the 1960s is not that the end is near but that it is now. Now is the time of judgment.

The end of time occurs now, and *The Moving Target* culminates in "For Now," a poem of departure like the first poems in the book but much richer because it embodies the book's accumulated insights. "For Now" has its roots in an ambitious autobiographical epic called "Congé" (a word that means taking one's leave), which Merwin never completed. By the time it becomes "For Now," Merwin "has understood that this work must be a reciting of everything he wishes to place behind him."[21] The recitation is urgent: "You are not here will the earth last till you come / I must say now what cannot / Be said later Goodbye" (MT, 89). The list of goodbyes is long. "Goodbye iron Bible containing my name in rust," "Goodbye pain of the past that / Will never be made better" (MT, 91), "Goodbye to the dew my master" (MT, 92). The recitation contains hints of the past, as in "Goodbye faces in stains churches / In echoes" (MT, 89), whose roots *Unframed Originals* locates in a recollection from childhood.[22] It also contains hints of the future, as in "Goodbye anniversaries I pass without knowing," a line that anticipates "For the Anniversary of My Death" (L, 58).

Most importantly, though, "For Now" clarifies the impor-
tance apocalypse has for Merwin: it is a means of evaluation.
"Tell me what you see vanishing and I / Will tell you who you are"
(MT, 93). "For Now" is Merwin telling us what he sees vanishing.

> Goodbye what we may never see
> Age would have kissed false teeth if any
> Its caresses making a bed slowly
> Even as a child I hoped it would spare me
> I made tears for it I sang
>
> As the cards are laid out they turn to ashes
> I kiss
> The light to those who love it it is brief
>
> Goodbye before it is taken away[.] (MT, 94)

Here Merwin "bids goodbye to all that is past and passing," which
includes something apocalypse demands, something that foreshadows his new ecological perspective in *The Lice:* "at the end
of the poem he says goodbye to all that is human."[23] Although he
will return to the human by the time he writes *The Compass
Flower,* "for now" he is moving as far as one human can move
from the rest of humanity.

"For Now" confirms "the authoritative vantage point the
poet has attained, from which he is able to distinguish between
what is inevitable and what is imposed, between the necessities
that are unavoidable and so must be embraced and those that were
invented by his culture and his upbringing and that would impose

shackles."[24] That vantage point lends its authority to Merwin's next—and arguably his greatest—book, *The Lice.*

The Moving Target prepares for *The Lice* by locating the "intuition of apocalypse" that is, "as all the reviewers of *The Lice* have declared, its first premise." But if apocalypse is the first premise of *The Lice,* it is also the first premise of any number of other books in the 1960s: "What makes *The Lice* special in a decade of writing that will be remembered for its apocalyptic obsessions, is an eerie sense of bearing witness to a world already in mid-apocalypse. These are not portentous poems so much as notations on the experience that it is all but over and done with, that we are merely 'the echo of the future,' and 'tomorrow belongs to no one.'"[25] *The Moving Target* reveals how Merwin's sense of apocalypse develops from the application of his tragic vision to history; the next chapter will find in *The Lice* a different consequence of his tragic vision.

It is not clear, after all, why there should *be* a book after *The Moving Target.* Why would anyone who is convinced of the imminence—indeed the presence—of the end continue to write? One of Merwin's answers to that question is simply that he *did* write,[26] but I think there is another answer as well. "Absolute despair," Merwin says, "has no art, and I imagine the writing of a poem, in whatever mode, still betrays the existence of hope, which is why poetry is more and more chary of the conscious mind, in our age. And what the poem manages to find hope for may be part of what it keeps trying to say" (RM, 297). Hope, in Merwin's case, is equivalent to purpose, and he found a purpose in announcing humanity's self-destructiveness, especially in our self-destructive relationship to the natural environment.

CHAPTER FOUR

Ecology

"Whether one has lived in vain depends on what happens to the world. If it devours itself, one is devoured along with it. If it saves itself, one has contributed something to this salvation."[1] Although those are not Merwin's words, they sum up succinctly his sense of human responsibility toward our natural environment, and they explain the connection between his preoccupation with apocalypse and his equally pervasive preoccupation with ecology. Merwin recognizes that the threats to the earth and to humanity are not millennial religious threats but very real ecological ones. He is concerned with apocalypse as a destiny we are choosing for ourselves by our own actions, rather than as a fate to be imposed on us by an angry god. "I'm not talking about a big bang; I'm talking about something that is happening as we are sitting here talking about it—the destruction of the seas, the destruction of species after species, the destruction of the forests. These are not replaceable. We can't suddenly decide years down the line that we made a mistake and put it all back."[2]

Some contemporary biologists concur with Merwin's conjunction of apocalypse and ecology. Lynn Margulis and Dorion Sagan point out that

the lesson of the fossil past warns that superficially extremely successful life forms are often at the end of their biological tether. Historically, species just prior to their extinction often reproduce in considerable profusion. The many species of archeocyathids and trilobites in the Cambrian period, and of dinosaurs in the Cretaceous, are witness to this inauspicious process, which Meredith calls "devolution." As Charles Darwin realized, organisms adapt to their environment because of constant checks on their tendency toward unlimited growth. If they are not adapted they may decline in numbers and become extinct. But, according to Meredith, they may also become *too* adapted, multiply, deplete their resources, and *then* become extinct. . . . From the standpoint of Meredith's theory of devolution, it is easy to see that the implications of human population growth are not necessarily synonymous with progress.[3]

Merwin's ecological poetry continues the debunking of meliorism begun in *The Moving Target.*

Formulated in another way, in books such as *The Lice* Merwin is writing the poetry of human insignificance. A tragic vision applied to human history results in a sense of apocalypse; tragic vision applied to nature undercuts anthropocentrism. Tragedy recognizes that humans do not "have dominion over the fish of the sea, and over the fowl of the air, and over every living thing that moveth upon the earth," and that we never will. Floods and earthquakes and diseases have defied human control for as long as humanity has existed. Nature was not created for, and does not culminate in, humanity.

As a statement of human insignificance, his poetry finds justification in other areas of recent thought. To cite Margulis and Sagan again, "Human beings are not particularly special, apart, or alone. A biological extension of the Copernican view that we are not at the center of the universe deprives us also of our place as the dominant form of life on the planet. It may be a blow to our collective ego, but we are not masters of life perched on the final rung of an evolutionary ladder."[4] Margulis and Sagan argue that the "knowledge we have accumulated about *all* other species" indicates that the species homo sapiens "will be replaced with none, one, or two descendant species within a million years or so."[5] That knowledge indicates that we are in a "parasitic" stage like the early stages in the spread of a microbial invader, in which the microbe kills its host, and that our only hope of extending the life of the species is to learn (like the microbe) to be less damaging to our host. If a microbe kills its host too soon, it cannot spread, and it will die. The host of the parasite humanity is the earth.

Although his justifications are moral rather than scientific, Merwin's poetry implies a similar viewpoint.

> Man's superiority to the rest of creation and his right to hold over it the powers of life and death, evolution and extinction, are questioned scarcely more often or more seriously than they were when he boasted a soul as his excuse. Now in the rare instances where his convenience alone is not taken as ample justification for his manipulations and erasures of other species, it is his intelligence, or some aspect of it, that is held up most regularly as the great exoneration. This, according to the myth, was the property which gave him the edge on the other creatures; and in the process it became endowed, in his eyes, with a spontaneous moral splendor which now constitutes between him and the rest of nature not a relative but an absolute difference. (RM, 206)

ECOLOGY

One need look no farther among moral philosophers than among scientists to find views concurrent with Merwin's questioning of human superiority to nature. Iris Murdoch says that "our minds are continually active, fabricating an anxious, usually self-preoccupied, often falsifying *veil* which partially conceals the world" but which overestimates our importance in the world. In her view, "anything which alters consciousness in the direction of unselfishness, objectivity and realism is to be connected with virtue." Like Merwin, she spells out her moral view in artistic and ecological terms: "I am looking out of my window in an anxious and resentful state of mind, oblivious of my surroundings, brooding perhaps on some damage done to my prestige. Then suddenly I observe a hovering kestrel. In a moment everything is altered. The brooding self with its hurt vanity has disappeared. There is nothing now but kestrel. And when I return to thinking of the other matter it seems less important."[6] She is morally obligated, in other words, to resist overestimating her own importance and by extension that of humanity. Similarly, Joseph Brodsky says that when your existence is in "its proper perspective," the result is "precision and humility. The former, it must be noted, breeds the latter. The more you learn about your own size, the more humble and the more compassionate you become to your likes, to the dust aswirl in a sunbeam or already immobile atop your table."[7] The "proper perspective" for humans is both precise *and* humble; it cannot be the former without being the latter.

The absence of the precision that breeds humility is just what Merwin has noticed in the human species, and it is in that absence of humility that Merwin's apocalyptic and ecological concerns unite: "*The Lice* was a book that was written for the most part when I felt the historic future was so bleak that there was no point in writing toward it. One element of the feeling in that book is still with me—the amazement at the terrible arrogance of our own species, which is certainly the most destructive on the planet. What we are prepared to do, to ensure our comfort and convenience, to the rest of the world—to the trees, to other cultures, with nuclear weapons or whatever!"[8] The future is bleak because our species is arrogant, and arrogance creates self-deception: our pride in the number of bushels of corn we can get one acre of soil to yield leads us to ignore the number of acre-feet of topsoil we are destroying by our farming methods.

Merwin studiously avoids explicitly topical poems. The practiced mythmaker knows that the most powerful and lasting literature cannot be *only* topical, and he thinks we have the necessary background information to make myths topical without his having to do it for us: "you know the story without me giving the details: the destruction of the wolves in Alaska, the actual changing of the climate, the wrecking of the water table, what's happening to the atmosphere, the things that we put in it that go round and round the planet, changing the atmosphere itself, including nuclear waste. Things that we don't even know about until long afterwards."[9]

Human arrogance is the starting point for "The Last One": "Well they'd made up their minds to be everywhere because why not. / Everywhere was theirs because they thought so" (L, 10). "Their" arrogance in the poem gets defined as "our" arrogance in this comment from an interview: "The way we've grown up, we take it for granted that when there's a forest you destroy the forest.

The first thing you do with trees is cut them down. You do something else then, you make fields out of them, but you don't leave the forest alone. Having gotten rid of the forest, you get rid of it over and over, and all you have left is this spindly growth. Then you bulldoze it away and then you strip-mine it. By the time you've done that, everything that was there, any culture it could have supported, any complexity of biological growth, any life of any kind, has just been cut out of the way."[10] In the poem, once "they made up their minds," they "started to cut," and "they cut everything because why not." The poem rejects the American ideal embodied in the idea of "manifest destiny" and given literary formulation in the poetry of Walt Whitman. Merwin sees that ideal not only as destructive of the continent, but also as self-destructive, so he constructs not a creation myth but a de-creation myth. He watches as "they" cut until they come to the water, but then he watches as "the last one" responds.

Or, more precisely, as its shadow responds. They can cut down the last one, but they cannot eliminate its shadow. "It is not *nature* gaining her revenge so much as nature's *shadow*—a hollow, dark force of non-nature, of obliterated nature, a dark, non-palpable reminder of what used to be. It is the lack of nature that creeps back over the continent, obliterating man. It is the exhaustion of natural resources that causes the machines to cease functioning and leads man back to a primitive state, forced once again to use sticks and his hands, because there is no energy left for his machines."[11] They try everything they can to destroy the shadow, but they fail. They try lights, explosives, and fire; they try to bury it, to ignore it, to dry it up. But always "The shadow stayed where it was before. / It went on growing it grew onto the land" (L, 11). The shadow takes the same destructive trail they had blazed, but in the opposite direction, destroying them as they had destroyed the trees.

> They began to stomp on the edge it got their feet.
> And when it got their feet they fell down.
> It got into their eyes the eyes went blind.
> The ones that fell down it grew over and they vanished.
> The ones that went blind and walked into it vanished.
> The ones that could see and stood still
> It swallowed their shadows.
> Then it swallowed them too and they vanished. (L, 11–12)

If ever one of Merwin's poems had a moral, this is it, and the moral is that "Americans think they have conquered the wilderness, only to find that No-Wilderness will conquer them."[12]

After "The Last One" envisions the destruction of humanity, "The Widow" imagines what the world will look like without us, discovering that the world "seems to get along very nicely without" humanity: "It is only the man-made impositions on nature that are fragile, that will fade; life itself goes on smoothly without man's aid."[13] In contrast to our imagined importance, for the widow "There is no season / That requires us" (L, 34). Our persisting in the belief that we are important has nothing to do with the facts; it is only an expression of our desires: "You grieve / Not that heaven does not exist but / That it exists without us." As if to follow up on his earlier lines "Tell me what you see vanishing and I / Will tell you who you are" (MT, 93), Merwin says in "The Widow" that "Everything that does not need you is real" (L, 35).

Even human reality, "The Widow" implies, comes less from humanity than from animality, from being part of nature, an idea developed in "A Scale in May," in which a speaker who first learns from humanity moves to learning from nonhuman nature. The poem is in eight sections, corresponding to the eight notes in a musical scale, but "the first four sections or notes of the poem deal with man; the last four, with the exception of line 17, deal primarily with nature. The dichotomy in the poem is between the human and the nonhuman, between the verbal and the nonverbal."[14] In the first four, human artifacts appear: doorways, songs, watches, ballots, kingdoms, temples. In the second four, the objects are predominantly natural: stars, light, an owl, petals, shadows. Only by resuming his place within nature, instead of trying to rule over or rise above nature, can the speaker "read what the five poplars are writing / On the void" (L, 50).

If the biological law that "ontogeny recapitulates philogeny" is true, then Merwin's ecological preoccupation might be expressed in terms of specietal maturation: the species is now recognizing its own mortality. That recognition receives its most dramatic rendering in "For a Coming Extinction" (L, 68). The title appears to refer to the coming extinction of the "Gray whale" of the first line, which "we are sending" to "The End / That great god," but the recognition gradually dawns on the reader that it refers also to the coming extinction of humans, "we who follow you." Merwin sees an interconnectedness in all life that not only makes the extinction of humans follow inevitably from the extinctions we are causing but also makes the extinctions equivalent. The coming extinction of the gray whale is not tragic *because* it implies the extinction of humans, nor is the coming extinction of humans either more or less tragic than any other extinction: each coming extinction is tragic because it irreplaceably removes something from the whole in which all species have their being. Merwin related his ecological concerns to this whole while discussing "For a Coming Extinction" at a 1987 poetry reading:

> I was in college when the bomb dropped. I have never been able . . . since those days to make a distinction I believed in between the part of us that craves the arts, craves poetry, cares about it, is obsessed with it, and the caring about other cultures, other languages, other kinds of life. I don't think of them as causes. I think of them as so intimately related that if you don't see them as a whole, you're simply missing part of it, and I think that if you pick up part of it everything else comes with it. I don't think that people have duties to take up particular causes; I think that if you care about any of these things, somewhere it's implied that it means something about how you feel about the rest of them. . . . I can't imagine that someone who reads Yeats with passion would sit back happily and watch a Caterpillar tearing up the redwood forests forever.[15]

The form his ecological concerns take is dictated by his tragic vision: because "every object includes the universe in its constitution and the laws of its being,"[16] our murder of the gray whale is also a self-inflicted wound.

This poem places humans and whales as inseparable and equivalent parts of a larger whole, but this "latest in Merwin's pod of whale poems"[17] is more complex and ambiguous than that description alone indicates. For one thing, this poem "owes something to Jonah and Job."[18] Merwin could have chosen any of the hundreds of species then threatened with extinction, but his choice of the whale was governed in part by his propensity for myth. The whale brings with it into the poem echoes of a rich literary history: it has been the instrument of divine punishment in the biblical book of Jonah, an instance of the limits of human understanding in the book of Job, a symbol of the link between nature and fate in *Moby Dick,* and so on.

For another thing, "care" is hardly the only state of mind in the poem. The narrator may care about other kinds of life, but he also "takes a coolly savage satisfaction in the proposal that our driving whales to 'the black garden' is only a logical antecedent of our own doom."[19] Nor is the inextricability of any species from the whole of nature the only idea in the poem. As soon as he says that "we who follow you invented forgiveness / And forgive nothing," the narrator "finds himself in deeper philosophical waters than those traversed by the animal. He asks forgiveness while simultaneously realizing that [the] very notion of forgiveness is a human projection. . . . To invent forgiveness is to invent history."[20]

Finally, the speaker is made intentionally unreliable. Like the "Cretan Liar" logicians puzzle over or the speaker in James Tate's poem "The Book of Lies," the speaker here formulates his own dishonesty: "I write as though you could understand / And I could say it / One must always pretend something / Among the dying" (L, 68). That ambiguity in the speaker renders ambiguous his attitude toward the "irreplaceable hosts" that have been "Our sacrifices": is he sorry about their extinction or not? is his tone ironic or serious? and does he really mean it when he asks the whale to "Join your word to theirs / Tell him / That it is we who are important" (L, 69)? If "The Last One" communicates an explicit moral, "For a Coming Extinction" displays more subtlety: it forces the reader to confront his own immediate reaction, which is "to destroy people who think like this speaker."[21] The reader sees his own impulse as no less destructive than those he blames.

The fact that frequently recurring natural phenomena like hurricanes and earthquakes should count for humans as "disasters" shows how tenuous is the species' existence. Humans think of themselves as rulers of the earth, but in fact we are utterly dependent on it and subject to its every whim. "It's seen as an object of exploitation, rather than as something of which we are a part. We are neither superior nor inferior, we are a part of it. It is not different from us. So when we treat it with contempt and exploit it, we are despising and exploiting ourselves."[22] *The Lice* begins the process of overcoming that contempt by identifying with animals: "Animals naturally embody that unknowing state which becomes, for Merwin, the condition of sensitivity to the spirit of the world."[23] Identification with animals prompts the realization Camus advocates: "If man realized that the universe like him can love and suffer, he would be reconciled."[24] Even in poems like "Death of a Favorite Bird" and "Fly," in which Merwin speaks in the voice of a human, he manages to identify with the animal in question, deeply enough that he becomes if not the pigeon itself then the pigeon's death: "So that is what I am" (L, 73). Even poems that try to identify with animal consciousness pursue the Socratic ideal of self-knowledge. In *The Lice,*

ECOLOGY

Merwin, having abandoned other authorities like society and gods, asks the earth to tell him what he is.

It answers as inscrutably as did the Delphic oracle. Merwin knows to avoid the most common form of human neglect of endangered species, which considers only the consequences of the threatened extinction for human welfare. But the humble view of humans which accepts our insignificance to the whole of nature must also recognize the insignificance of other species. Ninety-eight percent of all species that have ever lived are extinct. If humans are not important, neither are other species, so human insignificance provides no reason for trying to protect them. Considered in this way, a person's life resembles that of a protagonist in a tragedy: forces more powerful than the person will have their way, but that does not eliminate his self-interest or his suffering. "In Autumn" captures this tragic view of nature. "The extinct animals," Merwin reports, "are still looking for home / Their eyes full of cotton" (L, 41), but they will never find it. The stars come out, in complete indifference to the earth. Yet their indifference does not cause indifference in the speaker. The lights in the leaves remain "cities / Where I had hoped to live" in spite of the stars' indifference and in spite of the extinctions.

As a "pure homage to nature" the poems in *The Lice* "are unsuccessful. Merwin's awareness of his humanity intrudes upon them, at first bitterly, then with a grudging acceptance. . . . Such intrusions are necessary if he would emerge from his withdrawal. The idea of paying homage to nature would be no different from a disgusted dismissal of the affairs of our species. But he understands he cannot retreat."[25] He understands, in other words, that he *is* human and that his humanity and his attitude toward nature combine to alienate him both from other humans and from nature. As a human, his inevitable, tragic complicity in the human destruction of the rest of nature separates him—unintentionally—from other species, yet his attempt to identify with animal consciousness separates him—intentionally—from other humans. This sense of being caught between two worlds is captured in "My Brothers the Silent" (L, 78). His alienation from other humans is expressed in his questions to his brothers:

> What are you afraid of since I was born
> I cannot touch the inheritance what is my age to you
> I am not sure I would know what to ask for
> I do not know what my hands are for
> I do not know what my wars are deciding
> I cannot make up my mind[.]

He knows that he has "the pitiless blood and the remote gaze of our lineage," but at the same time he recognizes that his is an uncharitable family in which he is not welcome. Animal consciousness does not save him, though, from this alienation.

> Even your sheep our sheep
> When I meet them on the roads raise toward me
> Their clear eyes unknowable as days
> And if they see me do not recognize me do not
> Believe in me[.]

No simple solution emerges from *The Lice*.

One of the specific consequences of Merwin's apocalypticism has been his deepened appreciation of nature. This same conjunc-

ECOLOGY

tion between apocalypse and ecology will reappear throughout his work. In *The Lice,* the poems are often volatile, expressing his love for nature largely through anger and despair, but in his later works the tone will be anger less often than wonder mixed with mournfulness. In that sense, "Looking for Mushrooms at Sunrise" (L, 80), the last poem in *The Lice,* anticipates the shape his ecological concerns will take in future works. Its lamentation for "centuries of dead chestnut leaves" and its wonder at "the oriole / Out of another life" and the "gold chanterelles" conjoins apocalypse and ecology just like such later works as this description of an experience while camping in Baja.

Late in the afternoon, some of the sea birds make their last dives for fish, and the pelicans resume their formations as though they were about to depart on a long journey. A pair of frigate birds dives again and again to within inches of the surface, trying to catch fish as they leap into the air. Then they gather with a dozen more frigate birds wheeling and playing in the thermals above the heated slopes of the hill just west of the bay. As the sun goes down, the sky and the water both turn a deep turquoise. Something splashes far out on the water. At the end of the bay the mountains are becoming shadows. I stand watching as though none of it might be there when I look again.[26]

CHAPTER FIVE

Society

In his 1995 commencement address at Harvard, Václav Havel identifies the disparity between scientific/technological development and moral stagnation as the fundamental problem facing human society. Human responsibility, he says, "seems incapable of keeping pace with civilization and preventing it from turning against the human race."[1] Our power to destroy ourselves, to incur guilt, exceeds our power to choose and enact what is good and beneficial. Havel shares this vision with Sophocles and Merwin, and his articulation of it helps to reveal the framework common to *The Lice* and *The Carrier of Ladders* by inferring a *political* imperative that closely resembles Merwin's depiction of *ecological* obligation. Havel says, "we must divest ourselves of our egotistical anthropocentrism, our habit of seeing ourselves as masters of the universe who can do whatever occurs to us. We must discover a new respect for what transcends us: for the universe, for the earth, for nature, for life, and for reality. Our respect for other people, for other nations, and for other cultures, can only grow from a humble respect for the cosmic order." He might as well be writing a commentary on Merwin: the same tragic vision that informs Merwin's view of history in *The Moving Target* and his view of nature in *The Lice* informs his view of society in *The Carrier of Ladders*.

Harold Bloom and Marjorie Perloff have criticized Merwin for his apocalypticism on the grounds that his predictions of the end have proven inaccurate: thirty years after the publication of

The Lice, people are still writing poems, still living in a world full of animals, and still reading Merwin. Such criticism misconstrues Merwin's 1960s apocalypticism as a prediction of historical events (or as a prediction of the end of history altogether). But as chapter three shows, Merwin's apocalypticism is not a prediction but an evaluation, one to which Merwin's recent writings indicate he is still committed, and one that remains compelling. Bloom's criticism reveals its own weakness: "The pressures of the quasi-apocalyptic nineteen-sixties have made of Merwin an American Orphic bard," but "no poet legitimately speaks a Word whose burden is that his generation will be the very last. Merwin's litanies of denudation will read very oddly when a fresh generation proclaims nearly the same dilemma, and then yet another generation trumpets finality."[2] But every generation is quasi-apocalyptic, because visions of the end are one of the best ways to think through to their culmination the consequences of the present, so powerful apocalyptic visions retain their interest for "fresh generations" no less than do other powerful works of literature. The interest of Merwin's apocalyptic poetry is not limited to the 1960s any more than the interest of *The Scarlet Letter* is limited to Puritans. Both evaluate human society.

This is not to say that Merwin's apocalyptic poetry about human society does not fail, only that Merwin himself states more accurately than Bloom or Perloff the sort of failure and the reason for it.

The decision to speak as clearly and truthfully and fully as possible for the other human beings a poet finds himself among is a challenge to obscurantism, silence, and extinction. And the author of such a decision, I imagine, accepts the inevitability of failure as he accepts the inevitability of death. He finds a sufficient triumph in the decision itself, in its deliberate defiance, in the effort which it makes possible, the risks it impels him to run, and in any clarity which it helps him to create out of the murk and chaos of experience. In the long run his testimony will be partial at best. But its limits will have been those of his condition itself, rooted, as that is, in death; he will have recognized the enemy. He will not have been another priest of ornaments. (RM, 291–92)

Merwin's testimony in *The Carrier of Ladders* is partial, but it is not the poetry of "a priest of ornaments."[3]

Merwin's poetry of the 1960s culminates in *The Carrier of Ladders* (1970), the volume for which he was awarded the Pulitzer Prize and in which what Merwin has to say about human society figures most prominently. These are political poems, but not in the sense of making explicit reference to contemporary public figures or events: specific references more typically name historical figures like William Bartram and Andrew Jackson than contemporary figures like Richard Nixon, and historical events like the removal of Native American tribes from the eastern United States across the Mississippi rather than contemporary events like the Vietnam War. As his apocalyptic vision aims for a mythic scope that will keep it relevant to "fresh generations," so his social criticism seeks a mythic scope that will make it more than merely occasional. "The president of lies" (CL, 57) may have referred to Richard Nixon for early readers of *The Carrier of Ladders,* but it surely referred as meaningfully to Ronald Reagan for later readers.

Merwin's aversion to explicit reference to contemporary events is by conscious design. He says, "I don't see why public events" cannot prompt political poems, but "I think they probably do it rather seldom, in comparison with the number of times that they touch off the *intention* to write poetry or anything else, which of course isn't remotely the same thing. No, I've no principle against political poems. I just wish, sometimes desperately, that mine or anyone else's turned out more often to be poetry. . . . But in the main I think poetry itself remains political, and will do so more and more, by remaining the expression of the authentic, which is of course necessarily individual, in an age that is the enemy of anything of the kind."[4] To the extent that human nature transcends geopolitical boundaries and shapes political events, any "expression of the authentic" will retain its force as a social criticism.

Merwin's evaluation of society is linked to his ecological views, and in this his model is Henry David Thoreau.[5] Merwin sees himself in terms similar to the "I" in *Walden,* who has "lived alone, in the woods," for "two years and two months," in "a house which I had built myself," but who says that "at present I am a sojourner in civilized life again."[6] Similarly, Merwin lived for many years in the house in France that he refurbished, but he could not keep himself from coming back to New York and sojourning in "civilized" (or at least urban) life again. Also, Merwin holds some beliefs that resemble Thoreau's. For example, Thoreau says, "Most of the luxuries, and many of the so-called comforts of life, are not only not indispensable, but positive hinderances to the elevation of mankind. With respect to luxuries and comforts, the wisest have ever lived a more simple and meager life than the poor."[7] Merwin eschews certain luxuries and comforts, taking pride in his choice early in his career to live in modest housing in order to retain the freedom to write full-time and later building his home in tropical Hawaii without air-conditioning.

Because of this general affinity between the two, many of the attitudes toward society embodied in Merwin's poetry will resemble those expressed by Thoreau. So when Thoreau says "The civilized man is a more experienced and wiser savage" (40); "Most of the stone a nation hammers goes toward its tomb only. It buries itself alive" (58); or "if we stay at home and mind our business, who will want railroads?" (92), it is reasonable to expect similar views in Merwin.

The Lice is arranged chronologically, passing from season to season through a year; *The Carrier of Ladders* is arranged geographically, passing from east to west across the North American continent like the Native Americans being pushed westward or the sun passing east to west in a day. So the reader starts "toward morning" with a "dream of the first words / of books of voyages" (CL, 4) and passes from Lackawanna through Kansas to the Western Country, ending at an "Inscription Facing Western Sea" in a "Sunset After Rain." This passage east to west is also a passage through the darker side of United States history, the most prominent feature of which is the westward expansion of the country.

One who criticizes a society to which he or she belongs does so as a participant in that society and as one partially responsible for its current state. Further, just as any statement, even a statement of grief, implies at least a small amount of hope, so any social criticism implies an affirmation of the society being criticized: beneath my objection to a congress that would take away government funding for the arts and humanities while subsidizing tobacco farmers lies an affirmation of the democracy that empowers congress to do so.

Merwin certainly is aware of the ambiguous position dissent puts him in, and writes in "Envoy from D'Aubigné" an "indirect manifesto"[8] of dissent. An explanatory note that once accompanied the poem began, "Agrippe D'Aubigné, French Protestant poet, 1550–1630, soldier and courtier from the age of 18, served Henry IV with devotion and candor even after the latter bitterly disappointed him by abjuring the Protestant faith. D'Aubigné's great poem, *Les Tragiques,* on the subject of the wars of religion in France, was written when he was no longer a soldier, and when the cause of Protestantism in France seemed lost. This defeat, and what it implied to him, was the 'prison' of the latter part of his life."[9] Merwin's point of view shares D'Aubigné's advocacy of the losing side. In D'Aubigné's case this meant Protestantism; for Merwin it means Native Americans and what in his mind they represent, a life lived in harmony with the land rather than one dominated by machinery and acquisitiveness.

In the poem, D'Aubigné speaks to his *Les Tragiques,* though his words double as Merwin's own words to *The Carrier of Ladders.*

Go book

go
now I will let you

> I open the grave
> live
> I will die for us both
>
> go but come again if you can
> and feed me in prison[.] (CL, 34)

The poem is sent out into society, but its real mission is to return from society, because "as they / have forgotten / truth habitually / gives birth in private." Social criticism alters not the whole of society but only particular people, so D'Aubigné/Merwin bids the book do its work of selection: "if there is in you any / joy / may the good find it // for the others be / a glass broken in their mouths," or just as potently, "Book / burn what will not abide your light" (CL, 35). Brunner points out that "the message is lost on one group, while another group extracts a positive insight," and therefore it would be "an error to see poems of *The Carrier of Ladders* as optimistic or pessimistic: they are pinned agonizingly between denial and affirmation."[10]

Between denial and affirmation stands evaluation, the hard gaze Merwin's apocalypticism gave his poetry of the 1960s. What his view shows him is that America has structured its national conscience in a self-affirming way. One can put this observation in strictly economic terms, as did a recent *Atlantic* article. Its authors assert that the gross domestic product (GDP) skews our evaluation of the economy in destructive ways. Because gross domestic product counts all transactions as additions to the nation's wealth, it encourages such problems as crime and pollution. Crime, for instance, "has given rise to a burgeoning crime-prevention and security industry with revenues of more than $65 billion a year. The car-locking device called The Club adds some $100 million a year to the GDP all by itself. . . ."[11] Waste of natural resources is encouraged by the GDP, because instead of counting the disappearance of minerals or trees as a loss, as any business would do in its accounting, the GDP counts their disappearance as a gain. The authors assert that "much of what we now call growth or GDP is really just one of three things in disguise: fixing blunders or social decay from the past, borrowing resources from the future, or shifting functions from the traditional realm of household and community to the realm of the monetized economy."[12]

Merwin's terms of accounting are moral rather than economic, but his view is similar: we are still telling ourselves that we are profiting by our losses. Merwin sees the roots of the problem not in the idea of the gross domestic product, but in a vision of America embodied in Whitman. "It makes me extremely uneasy when [Whitman] talks about the American expansion and the feeling of manifest destiny in a voice of wonder. I keep thinking about the buffalo, about the Indians, and about the species that are being rendered extinct. Whitman's momentary, rather sentimental view just wipes these things out as though they were of no importance. There's a cultural and what you might call a specietal chauvinism involved" (RM, 321). The effects that concern him, though, are not much different from those the *Atlantic* article's authors cite. "Driving in the West . . . you see some pile of ditched cars, or a little place where they serve trash—deep-fried food, or something like that—and you think, in order to bring this about dozens of young men were sent off to die of leprosy in the leper colonies, or hundreds of Indians and thousands of buffalo were killed and the whole place has been poisoned for years in order to bring about this little pile of shit. And it's described in terms of the triumph of civilization. What kind of impossible lie is this that we're all subscribing to?" (RM, 330–31).

The scrutiny of that impossible lie is most intense in the "American sequence" that includes the poems from "The Approaches" through "The Removal."[13] "The Wheels of the Trains" begins with the stark image, familiar to everyone who has travelled through the Midwest and the West, of train wheels in rows on spurs at stations, waiting "unmoved in their rust / rows of suns / for another life" (CL, 43). The railroad was a symbol of American progress, uniting the land from coast to coast, but Merwin chooses to focus on an aspect of railways that, though no less real, is often left "unnoticed for years." By inaugurating fast interstate travel, railroads enabled a single person to duplicate the country's "manifest destiny" by travelling from the East Coast to the West. That genocidal journey, however, generated "holes in the hill / endless death of the sky / foreheads long unlit / illegibly inscribed."

"Lackawanna" internalizes history, viewing the source of the river near his boyhood home as within himself: "Where you begin / in me / I have never seen / but I believe it now" (CL, 44). His history and the history of America conflate, so that when he says "through the night the dead drifted down you / all the dead" (CL, 45), the dead to whom he refers are "the Indians, the vague memories of the past on this continent which are now barely recognizable,"[14] but they are also his own dead and his own deaths, the ones he has had to die to be reborn in this "Jordan" river.

From the Pennsylvania of "Lackawanna" Merwin moves westward to the Mississippi River in "Other Travellers to the River," which apostrophizes William Bartram, the "botanist, painter, ornithologist, and writer whose *Travels* (1791) helped inculcate the idea of the Noble Savage in the white man's mind."[15] It envisions Bartram standing "gazing out over the sire of waters / with night behind" (CL, 46) in the east, but moving inexorably westward. The night and the river alike bear off the empty flower of the day. Bartram, though, is depicted as the voyeur who watches as "the sounds of the earth / danced naked / thinking no one could see them."

In "The Gardens of Zuñi" the "one-armed explorer" is John Wesley Powell, who "becomes the emblem for Merwin of the white man's movement into the wilderness. Powell, a geologist and geographer, led the Geologic Survey (1881–94) that mapped out the West, imposed American lines upon the wilderness; it was while he was issuing these maps that Frederick Jackson Turner announced the closing of the frontier, the end of wilderness."[16] Powell's physical impediment becomes for Merwin a symbol of his spiritual defect. For all of his exploration, Powell "could touch only half of the country" (CL, 49). His one hand sent back lines (the lines of maps, lines of words on a page, lines of communication), but he could never accomplish his task, because it was self-defeating. Like anthropologists studying small-scale societies they purport to respect, his very presence corrupted what he sought to witness in its purity. So his "other hand / his scout"

> sent back no message
> from where it had reached
> with no lines in its palm
> while he balanced
> balanced
> and groped on
> for the virgin land

> and found where it had been[.] (CL, 49)

In "Homeland," the natural environment calls down a curse on Andrew Jackson, the president who oversaw the removal of eastern tribes of Native Americans into the West. When "the sun goes down / driving a stake / through the black heart of Andrew Jackson" (CL, 50), we are reminded of "the last one" taking its revenge on them "whom the birds despise" (L, 10). But the American sequence culminates in another echo of *The Lice:* there the earth had been portrayed metaphorically as a widow. In accordance with the shift in emphasis from nature to society in *The Carrier of Ladders,* the widow appears again, but this time as the Native American who has been widowed by the long, forced 'trail of tears':

> I will not walk
> from the house I warmed
> but they carry me through the light

> my blackening face
> my red eyes
> everywhere I leave
> one white footprint
> the trackers will follow us into the cold
> the water is high
> the boats have been stolen away
> there are no shoes
> and they pretend that I am a bride
> on the way to a new house[.] (CL, 62)

In contrast to the "black winter" of coal dust in Lackawanna, the widow leaves a white footprint, but in both cases the water that must be crossed is black and cold. "Merwin's descent ends here; the vacant rooms of the natives' deaths are vacant rooms in himself, too, as the Indian disappears from his imagination and he returns to the present. Unlike Gary Snyder in *Turtle Island,* Merwin does not return to the present replenished with native ways; he returns only with an affirmation of American destructiveness, of man's stupidity and inhumanity, and of an irreplaceable emptiness lying beneath this continent."[17]

The ambiguity of the dissenter finds its most accurate form in "Psalm: Our Fathers." There the repeated declaration of identity ("I am . . .") is contingent on history ("I am the son of . . ."), but it is also always qualified ("I am the son of . . . *but* . . ."). "I am the son of joy but does he know me / I am the son of hope but he ascends into heaven" (CL, 92). Finding no fixed doctrine that will satisfy him, Merwin cannot identify with either the removal of Native Americans or the destruction of the natural environment imposed by white culture, nor can he pretend to assume the identity of the removed native or the harried animal. So he chants a litany of ambiguity and homelessness:

I am the son of a shadow and I draw my blinds out of respect
    but I cleave uneasily to the light
I am the son of love but where is my home and where the
    black baptismal cup and the frightened eyes that would
    still come to the names I gave them
I am the son of the tribe of Apher which set up empty tents
    and camped where it could defend them and was remem-
    bered for them but I have discovered that the unknowable
    needs no defense[.] (CL, 92)

His vision of apocalypse means that "I am the son of ruins already among us" (CL, 96), but Merwin is nearing the time when he can say with less reservation that "at moments I have found hope beyond doubt beyond desert beyond reason."

That moment arrives with *The Compass Flower,* whose poems show how significant is the change in tenor that occurred in Merwin's poetry between 1970 and 1977. In section II of *The Compass Flower* all the poems deal with that paradigmatic concentration of society, New York City. "City," the first poem in the section, signals the change.

I have steered in through the tightening outskirts
in the morning crowd
I have undergone inspections been counted have believed
I have learned the streets like seasons

SOCIETY

I have forgotten whole years
but never have I seen it with so few people showing
not even at this hour before daylight so little traffic
never so like held breath[.] (CF, 25)

He sees things here as he has never seen them before, and peace
is what until now he has missed.

In earlier poems Merwin recognized ambiguities concerning the relation between human society and nature, but in "The
Rock" he begins to accept an ambiguity he has not previously
confronted: the city, the very heart of human destruction of
nature, is itself a part of nature. For a large percentage of the
citizens of the U.S., the city *is* our natural environment:

when we can love it happens here too
where we tremble
who also are running like white grass
where sirens bleed through us
wires reach to us
we are bottles smashing in paper bags
and at the same time live standing in many windows
hearing under the breath the same stone
that is ours alone[.] (CF, 28)

The observation that human society is not only part of the
history of nature but also part of nature itself leads him to the
central poem in this section, "St. Vincent's." There he begins by
"thinking of rain clouds" (CF, 34), but soon begins to understand
that he has trained himself to attend to nature, but not to the city:

"I consider that I have lived daily and with / eyes open and ears to hear / these years across from St. Vincent's Hospital" without attending to it. Instead he "learned not to hear" the "sirens' howling nearer through traffic on / Seventh Avenue." He begins to list what observations he can recall, but they enforce an acknowledgment of how little he knows:

> I have known them all less than the papers of our days
> smoke rises from the chimney do they have an incinerator
> what for
> how warm do they believe they have to maintain the air
> in there
> several of the windows appear
> to be made of tin
> but it may be the light reflected
> I have imagined bees coming and going
> on those sills though I have never seen them
>
> who was St Vincent[.] (CF, 36)

The closing line "becomes at once a compelling question about forgotten origins, and in its answer an implicit but intense self-criticism. For St. Vincent was (is) precisely the patron saint of works of charity. . . . He also founded the Daughters of Charity, one of the first female orders to move from the cloister out into the world to do good works; in this poem the nurses who 'ray out' from the hospital recall them. This love and engagement are precisely what the speaker has lacked, and what Merwin rejected in the harsher poems of the sixties, where he chose instead to 'celebrate . . . our distance from men'" (L, 56).[18]

In "St. Vincent's" Merwin manages to transform his evaluation of society into a self-evaluation, and in so doing effects a transition in his poetry from public concerns (myth, apocalypse, ecology, society) to private concerns (love, family, and the two places, Hawaii and France, that he transforms into his own inner landscape).

CHAPTER SIX

Love

The claim, often advanced by theoreticians and teachers of literature, that death, God, and love are the only three subjects about which to write may be misleading, but it would be accurate to say that nearly every poet has written about at least one of those subjects, love. From Sappho to Gjertrud Schnackenberg, John Keats to Galway Kinnell, poets are drawn to love like June bugs to porch lights, and Merwin is no exception. In his case, love poems are sprinkled throughout his corpus, but they are most prominent in *The Compass Flower* and *Finding the Islands*. It is no mere coincidence that, of all Merwin's books, those are also the two most widely condemned by critics.

The reason most frequently given for the failure of those two books is the transition from negation in books like *The Lice* and *Carrier of Ladders* to affirmation in *The Compass Flower:* "Merwin sometimes [in the later books] attempts to write positively about love and nature, but regularly fails. Straightforward affirmation is a mode Merwin may never be able to recover. . . . In Merwin's case the impulse toward affirmation should be resisted. . . . The pain cannot be mastered or transformed."[1] To put this another way, if Merwin's second four books of poems were valid, then the ninth and tenth cannot be; if the world is as bleak a place as *The Lice* indicates, then the love celebrated in *The Compass Flower* cannot redeem it.

In a world ruled by a beneficent god or one where human society consistently progresses, love may be a sufficient force to redeem the world. But in a tragic world, in which malevolent or indifferent forces more powerful than ourselves influence human activity, love, no matter how strong, cannot redeem the world. If lovers can be parted by forces they cannot control, such as death, love may be a consolation, but it cannot provide security. If the world is tragic in the sense I have attributed to Merwin in chapter three, love does not keep it from being tragic.

The incompatibility between love and Merwin's tragic vision does not suddenly appear, though, with *The Compass Flower.* Charles Altieri observed it already in *The Moving Target,* the volume in which Merwin's bleak vision took shape. Altieri discusses "The Way to the River," a poem that concludes

> *Oh Necessity you with the face you with*
> *All the faces*

This is written on the back of everything

But we
Will read it together[.] (MT, 77)

He says the poem fails because "it ultimately relies on love—a phenomenon simply asserted by Merwin and hard to reconcile with most of his landscape. Conceptually, love seems too easy, too traditionally an emblem of the union of the personal and the whole (since love is potentially universal) to resolve displacements as disturbing as Merwin's despairing poems."[2] So Merwin's incorporation of love into his poetry has been a weakness throughout his mature books, because rather than investigating the possibility and the place of love in a barren landscape, Merwin treats it as a magical escape. When in *The Compass Flower* and *Finding the Islands* love becomes a central preoccupation rather than merely an occasional respite, the volumes as a whole become correspondingly weak.[3]

His love poems have not always suffered from this malady. Merwin's vision in the first four books is not yet so bleak that love is inconsistent with it, and the love poems themselves contain hints of self-doubt. For instance, "When I Came from Colchis" (FF, 72) not only fits with the mythical tenor of the rest of *The Dancing Bears,* but it also registers the same self-doubt Shakespeare's seventeenth sonnet raises: "Who will believe my verse in time to come, / If it were fill'd with your most high deserts?" Merwin's question is formulated in the last stanza:

> Now if, amazed, I come
> From the deep bourn of your hand,
> A stranger up from the sunned
> Sea of your eyes, lady,
> What fable should I tell them,
> That they should believe me?

In addition to their coherence with their sister poems, Merwin's early love poems have a music, generated by their metrical form, that suits their content. In contrast, the open form Merwin devised for his later books better suits anger and despair than love.

Merwin's own view of language ought to have served as a warning against the kind of love poems he wrote in *The Compass Flower* and *Finding the Islands*. In an interview, he asserts the inability of language to express love: " . . . the invention of language was the greatest single accomplishment of the human race.... Yet, at the same time, language is completely inadequate. ... When you are in love with someone, or when a friend dies, or when you are angry with someone, words fail completely.... So language is both great and poor. The language of poetry is to be found in between."[4] When the narrator speaks about other themes in the middle four books, he is very self-conscious about the inadequacy of language, but when Merwin writes the love poems in *The Compass Flower* and *Finding the Islands* the narrator displays no equivalent self-consciousness, speaking instead as if words did not "fail completely."

At least two major problems, then, condemn the love poems from the outset: the inconsistency between them and the rest of Merwin's corpus, and the inconsistency between them and Merwin's view of language. But an examination of some of the poems will reveal other problems as well. We may start with "Kore," the long love poem in *The Compass Flower.* Kore was the name under which the Greek goddess Persephone was worshipped in Attica. She was the daughter of Zeus and Demeter, and was carried off by Hades, as whose consort she ruled in the underworld. Demeter asked Zeus to grant her release, to which he agreed on the condition that she must not have eaten anything while in the underworld. Since, as it turned out, she *had* eaten from a pomegranate Hades had offered her, Demeter had to be satisfied with a compromise by which Kore/Persephone would spend half the year (spring and summer) in this world and the other half in the underworld with Hades. In addition to specifying the goddess, "kóre" is the Greek word for "maiden," and it refers to a type of sculpture depicting a draped young female figure.

The poem is in twenty-four sections, each designated by a letter of the Greek alphabet, and it begins with an appeal to the myth. The narrator identifies his beloved with Kore, describing her smile as "the boat / in which my sun rides under the earth" and lamenting that "waking without you / is the beginning of winter" (CF, 49). Identifying the beloved with Kore does not prevent the hyperbolic metaphor (the lover's smile as a boat that carries a sun, her breath as waves that carry the boat) and the pathetic fallacy (insisting that the lover's absence begins winter) from making the narrator seem childish and unreliable. A similar exaggeration pervades the whole poem, as for example in ν:

> I have loved you in the four capitals
> of four worlds before this one
> with its glass season
> and the nakedness of their light
> wakes me now
> and the burning that the year comes back for
> leaping the falls of its own
> changes. (CF, 53)

This passage exemplifies what Freud called the overvaluation of the sexual object, the tendency (strongest in the first stages of love) to be blind to the lover's faults and to exaggerate the lover's virtues. The poem is weak because the narrator cannot be trusted. His giddiness leads him to say things that are silly because they are so far from the truth (the first two lines) or is far from making sense (the last three lines). The problem is twofold: the identification of the beloved with a goddess is unconvincing, and the goddess herself is too heavenly for one who spends half her life in hell.

Many of the other stanzas are equally nonsensical. Stanza ζ, for instance, consists of a string of disconnected and incoherent statements:

> You slept all the way to the garden
> face in the boat of my hand
> and we came more than a century late
> to the closed gate
> and the song the laurel remembers in the dark
> the night flute always beginning again
> on the untrodden slope
> and where we walked in the streets then there was new wine
> announced with green boughs over doorways
> in the time of the statues. (CF, 50)

The first two lines are a mixed metaphor: if both of them are travelling to the garden, it is difficult to visualize how his hand could be a boat or to construe as meaningful its being a boat. In the third line, the question 'late for what?' is unanswered; similarly, in the last line the question 'what statues?' is unanswered. No connection is offered between her sleeping all the way to the garden and their being more than a century late, or between either of those and the song or the new wine. In a successful surrealist poem, the lack of explicit connection would itself be illuminating, because (as in a dream) plausible implicit connections could be inferred easily, but here no illumination occurs: all the implicit connections to be found or constructed are strained and implausible.

A few moments nearly redeem the poem, as when the narrator says, "it is cold in the house / and I burned up all the matches in the night / to look at you" (CF, 54). Though overly sentimental, this is at least a striking image that depicts the narrator's plausible psychic state rather than asking us to accept as true the deluded beliefs the narrator holds about the lover. In other words, it corresponds to a high schooler's saying "I like x more than I like anyone else," instead of "x is the most beautiful person in the world." The former is plausible, but statements like the latter dominate the poem.

The poem does fulfill a role in the larger structure of the book. *The Compass Flower* has a seasonal pattern, and "'Kore' is the transition between the sorrow of autumn and the joy of summer."[5] But playing a role in the overall scheme of the book does not forgive failure as an individual poem, and "Kore" is simply not strong enough to stand by itself.

Similar problems plague "Spring Equinox Full Moon" (CF, 59), a poem that consists of a litany of metaphors praising the lover's various parts: her thighs are "slender sunset shining shores," her fingers are "rolled fragrant leaves," her feet are "first drops of rain on a mountain." She has "morsel breasts" and a "melon navel." But one need only think back to earlier, better love poems to see why this poem fails. Andrew Marvell points out the lack of urgency in such praise. "Had we but world enough, and time," he says,

> My vegetable love should grow
> Vaster than empires and more slow;

LOVE

> An hundred years should go to praise
> Thine eyes, and on thy forehead gaze;
> Two hundred to adore each breast,
> But thirty thousand to the rest.

Lovers, though, cannot afford such leisure, since "time's wingéd chariot" is always "hurrying near." Whatever the flaws in Marvell's poem, and however disingenuous his narrator, his poem draws out the disingenuousness in Merwin's narrator, whose praise of his lover is too easy. An even more damaging revelation comes from Shakespeare's sonnet 130.

> My mistress' eyes are nothing like the sun;
> Coral is far more red than her lips' red;
> If snow be white, why then her breasts are dun;
> If hairs be wires, black wires grow on her head.
> . . . .
> I grant I never saw a goddess go;
> My mistress, when she walks, treads on the ground.
> > And yet, by heaven, I think my love as rare
> > As any she belied with false compare.

By ironically playing off of poems in praise of the beloved, Shakespeare reveals that praise of the sort Merwin permits himself in "Spring Equinox Full Moon" ("I want to think for six hours of your hair / which is the invention of singing" [CF, 60]) cannot be trusted.

Like all the poems in *Finding the Islands,* the love poems in the second section, "Turning to You," consist of three-line stanzas separated from each other by dividing marks but gathered into individually titled sequences. The form, a clear departure for Merwin from that of his preceding books, resembles English versions of the Japanese haiku, but Merwin has been careful to point out that, although "I was intrigued by the notion of the linked haiku that Basho and some of his disciples were writing, and that was what made me think of joining a series of them so that they played off against each other and made a larger whole,"[6] these poems are not haiku. It would be more accurate to find the antecedents of this form in Merwin's own formal experiments in poems from earlier volumes, like "A Scale in May" (L, 50) and "Signs" (CL, 116). The beginnings of the form can be traced even farther, to Merwin's manner of taking notes. The Merwin archive at the University of Illinois includes many notebooks and loose sheets filled with notes in Merwin's simultaneously neat and barely legible hand: very often these notes are in small "stanzas" of from one to three lines, separated by the dash that eventually appeared in "A Scale in May" and "Signs" and only later in *Finding the Islands.*[7]

The potential of the form is not fully realized, though, because the love poems in *Finding the Islands* are debilitated by flaws similar to those that mar the love poems in *The Compass Flower.* The first poem in the section, "To Dana with the Gift of a Calendar," begins on a wrong note, with the same disingenuousness that occurred in "Kore." The exaggerated declaration that "In the winter of the first month of every / year of my life I was / looking for you" (FI, 41) might be made to work if it were put into a context that infused it with irony or that established a dramatic tension, but as it stands it is simply a lie engendered by the same giddiness that drives "Kore." The second stanza is merely trite, without the freshness and force of language in Merwin's better poems. The third stanza, like the first, suffers from unchecked hyperbole: "when I am away from you un-counted / clouds of fish are calling in the seas / and nobody hears them." This is either the statement of an irrelevant fact (clouds of fish are always calling in the seas and nobody ever hears them—so what?) or another instance of the pathetic fallacy, believing that nature shares in and expresses the writer's emotions (fish are calling in the seas now *because* I am away from you).[8]

The problem of exaggerated pronouncements in the early stanzas is exacerbated because other stanzas are so banal. Imme-diately after saying the lovers "lie on the floor in each other's arms / and listen to the drums / and the wolves" (FI, 42), the narrator discloses such mundane facts as where the lover has left her sunglasses and the site of a recent bout of lovemaking. It is as if by such bathos Merwin had set out to prove William Gass's contention that "the sexual, in most works, disrupts the form; there is an almost immediate dishevelment, the proportion of events is lost; sentences like *After the battle of Waterloo, I tied my shoe,* appear."[9] The interest of the most notable stanza in the poem derives not from poetic merit but from appeal to a lurid tabloid curiosity in the reader. The third stanza from the end, "we are attacked / and we / are one," apparently refers to a conflict at a Buddhist enclave in Colorado that involved Merwin and the lover to whom these poems are addressed.[10]

As in *The Compass Flower,* these poems have occasional redeeming moments. For instance, "Turning to You" has some memorable images, as in the first stanza: "Seeing my shadow on the cloud / I have reached for your hand / and found it" (FI, 43).

Later in the poem an equally vivid simile appears: "After seven years / still we feed each other like birds / by the breaking waves" (FI, 44). In the end, though, the poems' weakness always comes through. The final stanza of that poem passionately declares, "I want to be buried / under your heart / where I was born" (FI, 45). Such a declaration is subject to an objection similar to the "but the world didn't end" criticism Bloom and Perloff leveled against Merwin's apocalyptic poetry: in fact, not long after the publication of the poems, Merwin separated from the person to whom they are addressed, and he is now married to someone else. The separation does not mean that the desire was not actual or that the statement of the desire was insincere, but it does imply that the desire was a passing fancy with little force or interest.

Merwin's love poems are not inevitably failures. The strength of most of his poetic corpus is that, in keeping with his tragic vision, Merwin usually fulfills Kant's ethical imperative not to make an exception of oneself: Merwin exempts himself neither from responsibility for what he sees ("So that is what I am" [L, 73]), nor from the consequences of what he sees ("I will take you with me the emptiness of my hands" [L, 55]), whether or not he could have changed things. In the love poems in *The Compass Flower* and *Finding the Islands,* though, Merwin's vision weakens. A poet who normally avoids self-deception falls into it. The love poems are moments of weakness, of self-indulgence. Merwin himself seems to recognize that the love poems forsake his ecological commitments, as when in "The Mountains" he declares that "I believed that after / the last tree fell / you would still be there" (FI, 55). Such a belief, that one's own lover will live longer than nature, is precisely the sort of self-deception Merwin seldom allows himself in his other poems, as if he had designed the contrast between the clarity of vision in the apocalyptic poems and the self-deception in the love poems to support Nietzsche's maxim: "Fear has promoted knowledge of men more than love has, for fear wants to divine who the other is, what he can do, what he wants: to deceive oneself in this would be disadvantageous and dangerous. On the other hand, love contains a secret impulse to see as much beauty as possible in the other or to elevate him as high as possible: to deceive oneself here would be a joy and an advantage—and so one does so."[11]

When he incorporates the love poems into the larger landscape of his vision, though, as he begins to do in *The Rain in the Trees,* he ceases to use them as escapes from the harshness of that vision, with better results. In fact, Alfred Corn thinks these love poems are *very* successful. He calls the love poems in *The Rain in the Trees* "probably the most moving in that genre written by anyone in this decade, an impression heightened, I'd say, by the reflection that Merwin is now in his sixties. He seems to have reinvented love poetry for our day."[12]

Corn's assessment is overly enthusiastic, but he is right that, unlike the love poems in *The Compass Flower* and *Finding the Islands,* those in *The Rain in the Trees* work. They manage to avoid the weaknesses of the earlier love poems. For instance, "Being Early" solves the problem of hyperbole. In both the earlier and the later love poems, Merwin wants to create a sense of love's timelessness, but in the earlier poem "Islands," addressing the lover whom he has just described as "islands / a constellation of flowers breathing on the sea" (CF, 64), he makes the disingenuous assertion that "all my life I have wanted to touch your ankle." Surely even a lover who wishes the statement were true knows better than to believe it. In contrast, "Being Early" tells the truth, and in so doing creates the very sense of timelessness that "Islands" fails to create. "When you were born / I was a small child in a city / and even if somebody had brought me news of you / I would not have believed them" (RT, 38). Instead of the hyperbolic 'I always loved you,' the narrator here suggests the plausible (and consequently also more powerful) 'I know now that my life was empty before I loved you.'

Similarly, "Before Us" conquers the problem of overvaluation of the sexual object. Unlike the earlier poems that praise the wonders of the beloved in ways that anyone with more emotional distance than the narrator can recognize as false praise, here the declaration of love consists of a statement of urgency that anyone with a sense of their own mortality will recognize as true. The narrator begins by lamenting all the time he and the beloved were apart: "You were there all the time and I saw only / the days the air / the nights the moon changing / cars passing and faces at windows" (RT, 30). He then generalizes that lament by describing it as characteristic of humanity to wake too late, just like his love for the beloved, saying that the love of the human species for the earth has been realized too late,

> when the Laughing Owls have
> long been followed by question marks
> and honeycreepers and the brown
> bears of Atlas
> the white wolf and the sea mink have not been seen
> by anyone living[.] (RT, 30)

LOVE

He celebrates the fact that he and the beloved have at last realized their love and that their love incorporates a love of the earth: "we wake together and the world is here in its dew / you are here and the morning is whole." Finally, in the tradition of petitions like Robert Herrick's "Gather ye rosebuds while ye may" and Andrew Marvell's "Now let us sport us while we may," not to mention Robert Creeley's more lighthearted "Take off your clothes, love, / And come to me,"[13] he urges himself and the beloved to seize the day:

> now we have only the age that is left
> to be together
> the brief air the vanishing green
> ordure in office tourists on the headland
> the last hours of the sea
> now we have only the words we remember
> to say to each other
> only the morning of your eyes and the day
> of our faces to be together
> only the time of our hands with its vexed
> motor and the note
> of the thrush on the guava branch in the shining rain
> for the rest of our lives[.] (RT, 31)

The love poems in *The Rain in the Trees* succeed where those in *The Compass Flower* and *Finding the Islands* failed, because they no longer contradict Merwin's other concerns. "Before Us" does not use love as a way of escaping from or denying the ecological threats to Hawaii; instead, it integrates love for another human being with love of a place. Indeed, as if to prove William Bronk's claim that "Love hasn't much / to do with whom,"[14] the narrator's posture toward his beloved bears a striking resemblance to his posture toward their environment: "Place" expresses the same urgency in regard to his environment that "Before Us" expresses in regard to his beloved.

Merwin was able very early in his career to express accurately and powerfully concerns like his sense of the mortality of the human species and his recognition of the destructiveness of human societies. Others of his concerns had to wait before his powers were equal to them. Wittgenstein says, "You cannot write anything about yourself that is more truthful than you yourself are. That is the difference between writing about yourself and writing about external objects. You write about yourself from your own height. You don't stand on stilts or on a ladder but on your bare feet. . . . Nothing is so difficult as not deceiving oneself."[15] Merwin seems to have had to endure the grief of his parents' deaths before he could attain the perspective he needed to produce his most powerful writing about the family. Certainly he had to approach his own mortality before he could attain the perspective he needed to write successfully about love.

CHAPTER SEVEN

Family

Merwin's voluminous autobiographical work does not have the confessional character that has been a staple of the genre since Augustine and Rousseau wrote autobiographies, even though confessional poetry was prominent in America by the time Merwin began explicitly to incorporate autobiographical content into his work. Confession operates through catharsis: by disclosing as much as possible, especially what one most wishes to hide, one purges oneself of uncleanness. Merwin does very little confessing, but assembles instead a personal history that works not by purging himself of his past but by ordering it. His use of autobiographical material shares its motivation not with the parishioner in the confessional whispering his sins to the priest, but with the genealogist in the library tracing her family tree.

Merwin's autobiographical writings, in fact, are less a record of his own actions and feelings than a family history—a record of his origins. In this way his autobiographical writings are continuous with his interest in myth. Asked in an interview (conducted in 1981, the year before the publication of *Unframed Originals*) whether he agreed that myths "are inevitably, in some sense, creation myths," Merwin replied that " . . . myths are touching the origin of everything. They are touching the original dimension of everything,"[1] including himself. Also, family history, like myth, is timeless: "Personal history is not recorded in time—it's always present."[2] Part of his continuing attraction to family history is his sense that parents, as one's own inescapable origin, are themselves "a myth that runs through the whole of one's existence, and I find myself writing about them. I keep trying to move away from the subject of parents, but the faster I try the more it keeps recurring. I guess they provide some sense of confluence, of returning and beginning."[3]

This pursuit of origins makes family, in Jarold Ramsey's view, "the central line of imaginative continuity" that runs through Merwin's career. "As odd as it may seem to bracket this unromantic poet with Wordsworth, there is in all of Merwin's books . . . a bedeviled impulse to discover how the Child is Father to the Man, how one's days are bound each to each by some form of natural piety."[4] The extent to which family concerns pervade Merwin's work has become clear only since the publication of *Unframed Originals,* a book that reveals "family poems where we had not seen them before," transforming "much of what seemed alien and distant" into something "troubling and close: prophecy and cryptic comments now seem collapsed into re-markable expressions of family experiences. . . . His career begins to feel much more placed and personal, much more concerned with family and national myths than with universal myths."[5] The mythic and the familial are less easily separable in Merwin than one would expect. This chapter will focus on the works in which family figures explicitly.

Merwin records his family history because he believes that without understanding his family he will not understand himself. Beginning with the bald declaration "I think I was cold in the womb," the speaker in "The Forbears" then decides that his brother (who died soon after birth) must also have been cold in the womb, like his grandfather John and the forbears who antedated John:

> I believe they quaking lay
> beforetime there
> dancing like teeth and I
> was them all foretelling me
> if not the name the trembling
> if not the time the dancing
> if not the hour the longing
> in the round night. (CL, 102)

Merwin shares his identity with those forbears: "I / was them all." They foretell, if not the particulars of his life (his name, time, and hour), the more important existential aspects (like trembling and longing).

In his earliest explicit family poems, Merwin is anxious to differentiate himself from his forbears rather than to identify himself with them. "The earlier poems," he said in a 1984 interview, "seem to be more distant than what I would write now. I wouldn't like to write from such a distance." Those earliest explicit family poems were "just a way of getting the arm warmed up for being able to write something else, and later on the writer will come back to that material and be able to do something with it."[6] Such a disparaging assessment, though, belies their importance: distance was exactly what Merwin needed in order to be able to write "something else," and *The Drunk in the Furnace,* the volume in which the first family poems appeared, was the pivotal volume in which he came to the end of his early manner and prepared for *The Moving Target*. Kenneth Andersen says that "With the advent of his family portraits in the latter half of *The Drunk in the Furnace* . . . , Merwin finally comes ashore from his early alienation."[7] But just the opposite is true: Merwin is only coming to see in these poems an alienation that prepares for the departure poems that begin *The Moving Target*.

"John Otto," for instance, "comes ashore" to family issues only to praise an ancestor for leaving his family. It tells of "John Otto of Brunswick, ancestor / On my mother's side, Latin scholar, / Settler of the Cumberland Valley, / Schoolmaster, sire of a family" (FF, 245), who one day in his "white age" walked away from his "home of eighty years or so / And what cronies were left" to "follow / The road out of the valley" on foot to Carlisle, a distance of approximately fifteen miles, "to die of fatigue there, at ninety-six." Merwin imagines his ancestor cresting the mountain between Blain and Carlisle:

> I can see Carlisle Valley spread below
> And you, John, coming over the hill's brow,
> Stopping for breath and a long look;
> I can hear your breath come sharp and quick,
> But why it was you climbed up there
> None of us remembers any more.

No one knows why John Otto climbed that hill, but the poem's closing rhetorical question tells us the motive Merwin attributes to him: "was it to look once again / On another valley green in the sun / Almost as in the beginning, to remind / Your eyes of a promise in the land?"

FAMILY

John Otto has become for Merwin a mythical figure who resembles Moses, the elderly figure who has led the way to the promised land, which he views from a hill before dying but never enters, or John Keats's "stout Cortez when with eagle eyes / He stared at the Pacific . . . / Silent, upon a peak in Darien."[8] John Otto's departure from his family sanctions Merwin's own departure, announced in poems like "Home for Thanksgiving" and "Lemuel's Blessing" in *The Moving Target.* Merwin's own search for "another valley," for "a promise in the land," finds in John Otto a predecessor with similar ambitions.

Calling "Grandfather in the Old Men's Home" a "very deliberate attempt to make a myth out of personal, private, and local material," Merwin explains that "my grandmother's generation was very fundamentalist Methodist and didn't believe in alcohol—I mean, there are those who believed that buttermilk was sinful because sometimes it had as much as two degrees in it. . . . My Grandfather was a pilot, so I'm told, on the Allegheny River and a legendary local drunk. And he was put into the old men's home by his sons."[9] The myth he creates from that material tells of "the danger of embracing the constant and absolute rather than the conditional and ambiguous."[10] His grandfather, who through life has tormented his grandmother by drunkenness, long absences, and dangerous unpredictability, has finally satisfied her: he is "gentle at last" (FF, 247). But she is too rigid, "wearing the true faith / Like an iron nightgown," and he pays a heavy price to satisfy her. "The fact that he can only attain such a condition through senility is a scathing attack on middle-class morality,"[11] and transforms this into a poem of departure, too, a vow not to become like "the children they both had begotten, / With old faces now, but themselves shrunken / To child-size again," who stood by their mother "Beating their little Bibles till he died."

The short-lived energy of the family poems in *The Drunk in the Furnace* prompts the departure in *The Moving Target.* "John Otto" and "Grandfather in the Old Men's Home" are expansive poems that move easily from a few facts to myth, but Edward J. Brunner points out that those poems were written while Merwin was in Europe. The poems he composed after his return to America, like "Grandmother Dying," contract to a much narrower scope, unable to escape the gravity of the facts,[12] with the result that his attack on the morality of those he portrays is no less scathing, but it is significantly less subtle. "Grandmother Dying" depicts a woman "who for ninety-three years, / Keeping the faith, believed you could get / Through the strait gate and the needle's eye if / You made up your mind straight and narrow" (FF, 249). Her physical disfigurement ("her wrenched back bent double, hunched over / The plank tied to the arms of her rocker / With a pillow on it to keep her head / Sideways up from her knees") suggests her disfigured soul. What Brunner calls "the blunt reality of actual family history, with its ancestors who could not be accommodated to Merwin's agenda for poetry,"[13] shows Merwin that he needs more distance before he can transform his family into myth. "The Drunk in the Furnace," the most powerful poem in the volume and his best single poem prior to *The Lice,* derives its powerful depiction of the milieu of Merwin's childhood from a character for whom there was no "real-life" model.

Not until *Unframed Originals* does Merwin attain the psychic distance he needs to create his myths directly and explicitly from family materials. He has endured by then "the first shock of maturity: a realization that home, where you grew up and be-longed—belonged with and without your own volition—no longer exists. The desire to return to it, the moment you know it no longer exists" (RM, 179). He knows his home is gone, so the desire to return to it replaces the desire to escape it and readies him to write what many consider his best book.[14] "Everything Merwin knows about world literature serves him as he renders justice to the dense particularity of a family history poised between the ordinary world of middle-class aspirations and repossessions, and the twilight world of initiation, concealment, and destiny—perhaps the three great mythic subjects."[15]

Just as earlier critics were ready to see myth as the key to Merwin's work, since the publication of *Unframed Originals* they have attached tremendous importance to family.

As Merwin discloses his regret and resentment at the truncation of this relationship [with his alcoholic paternal grandfather], he also partially exorcises the powerful ghost of a "shaming . . . hurtful" father (UO, 176), whose constant messages were restriction and self-control, and of whose approval the boy never felt sure. . . . This exorcism takes on profound significance in light of the parallels between the Merwin of the sixties and the Calvinist spirit: the personal reserve; the ontological guilt and self-condemnation; the sense of original separation and nostalgia for lost whole-ness; the distrust of language and of (Whitmanian) erotic impulses. Even the poet's powerful ecological warnings may descend in part from his father's constant strictures against touching anything.[16]

Like an exclusive focus on myth, fixation on family yields only a one-dimensional reading of multidimensional works, but *Unframed Originals* does clarify the pervasiveness of Merwin's concern with family history throughout his work. Its inevitable separation and death, combined with its universality, make family history an ideal vehicle for depicting a tragic vision.

Merwin's organizing principle in *Unframed Originals* is straightforward: "one of the main themes of *Unframed Originals* is what I was not able to know, what I couldn't ever find out," but "I felt if I could take any detail, any moment, anything I could clearly see, and pay enough attention to it, it would act like a kind of hologram. I'd be able to see the whole story in that single detail" (RM, 326). Each of the narratives tries to find that single, telling detail that sheds light on a whole range of events or even on an entire life.

In "Tomatoes," the first chapter of *Unframed Originals,* that telling detail is an apparently trivial incident that occurs in the garden at his grandfather's home when Merwin was nine years old. Nietzsche writes that "the unresolved dissonances between the characters and dispositions of the parents continue to resound in the nature of the child and constitute the history of his inner sufferings."[17] Or, to echo Merwin's Presbyterian past, "the iniquity of the fathers" is visited "upon the children to the third and fourth generation."[18] In "Tomatoes," Merwin tells the story of his father and uncle persuading their father to enter a nursing home. The child Merwin, who had been raised in the city, was entranced by his grandfather's garden. When his father and his uncle prepared to go inside to talk to his grandfather, a conflict occurred between his father and grandfather that became a prototype for an internal conflict that has troubled Merwin through his entire adult life.

The old man said that if I was to be kept waiting I had to be made at home. My father, cutting across what the old man said, told me to just wait right there and not touch anything and they would not be very long. But the old man persisted. "He won't do no harm," he said. And to me, with a sweep of his hand, "You help yourself to anything you please." He pointed to some tall, lush bushes with intricate curling leaves, the sunlight glittering on tiny glass spines all over their fronds and long stems, their dark shadows hiding their feet, and he asked me if I knew what those were.

"Sure he does," he insisted to my father, without waiting for me to answer. And to me he said, bending down to point, "Them's tomatoes." He pulled aside some of the leaves. "Some of them's ripe," he said. "You can eat them right now."

"No," my father said, shaking his head. "That's alright now." And to me he repeated, "You let them alone. Don't touch anything."

"They won't bother you," the old man told me. "One time people used to believe they would kill you. Deadly poison. You believe that? Thought you'd die if you ate one." He laughed. "But we know better now. You just help yourself, if you see anything you want." (UO, 5–6)

In this piece of personal history, the drama of the fall is reiterated, with Merwin playing the role of Adam/Eve, his father playing a strict God, and his grandfather playing a benevolent Satan. In his poems Merwin stays in that ambiguous position in the garden, needing to obey simultaneous and contradictory injunctions to touch and not to touch. In *The Lice* and *The Carrier of Ladders,* the lush garden is America, which he must not touch in order to leave natural and wild what is native, yet which he must touch if he himself is to enjoy those natural elements. In the books from *Opening the Hand* through *Travels,* the Eden is Hawaii, which he must not touch so as not to be another invading foreigner despoiling what is native to the islands, but which he must touch in order to *restore* what is native. He focuses on the incident in "Tomatoes" because it foreshadows one of the fundamental dilemmas of his mature life and work.

In "Mary," a recollection of his father's cousin, who lived with the Merwins for some time during his childhood, the detail is her giving him some cinnamon hearts. Mary's room was a mysterious place which he was forbidden by his parents to enter or "even to stand outside" (UO, 63), but "she invited me in there, one day, herself. She took it into her head. There was no one else in the house. She was minding me. Rules sometimes came adrift. She led me in and stood there, facing me, and I stood there. She was entertaining me. I listened to her breathe. The room was smaller than it looked from the outside, and smelled more." But it is not merely the injunction to stay out of Mary's room that she invites him to violate. Mary often talked of Lindbergh, and "the year that he flew the Atlantic I was born. What did that mean? Never take candy from strangers" (UO, 62), as in fact Merwin had once been tempted to do, when a strange man and woman offered him "white tablets stamped with the heads of thistles" one day when he was in the yard. On the day when she invited him into her room, Mary also offered him candy.

> Behind her on a shelf stood a huge glass jar, like the ones in the drugstore, half full of something red, the one bright color in the room. She turned around and took the lid off and fished out a few red things the size of newborn fingernails, shaped like hearts. She explained that they were the shape of hearts, just like real ones, but were candy. And she held them out to me. . . . She told me to go ahead. She said go on, they're cinnamon. Go on, they won't do no harm, they're cinnamon. I took one. It was exciting. Go on, take more, she said, there's nothing to them. Go on, eat one, she said, eat it right now. I had been thinking of saving them. She took one out of the jar and popped it into her mouth, to show me. Then she stuck her tongue out with the cinnamon heart melting on it, wet and shiny, and the middle of her tongue was bright red. . . . I put one of the hearts in my mouth and it burned. I told her, but she said never mind that, they was good. Wasn't they? And I nodded, and let it melt and burn, as she said to, while I watched her, but nothing else happened. As I went along the hall I opened my hand and saw that the other heart had made my palm bright red, like her tongue, and I put it away. (UO, 63–64)

Like the central incident in "Tomatoes," this is an initiation, and it enacts a drama that Merwin replays in his poems. This time, instead of the fall, it is the wilderness temptation,[19] in which the child Merwin plays the role of Christ and Mary plays the role of Satan. As Satan tempts Christ to throw himself down from the parapet of the temple, so Mary's room tempts Merwin: the reason for his being forbidden even to stand outside her room is that "it was at the head of the stairs, which I might fall down" (UO, 63). As Satan tempts Christ by taking him to a high mountain and showing him all the kingdoms of the world, so Mary's room tempts Merwin with "another landscape" and "another sky." And as Satan tempts Christ to eat, so does Mary. Unlike Christ, Merwin yields to temptation, and the drama of temptation will be replayed over and over in the poems. Sometimes temptation wins, as in the rebellious poems at the beginning of *The Moving Target* and the sensual poems in *Finding the Islands,* at other times propriety wins, as in poems like "The Day Itself" (T, 54), but in either case, it is the struggle between liberty and authority repeating itself over and over in Merwin's poems.

The crucial detail in "La Pia," Merwin's narration of his mother's life through the events leading up to her death, is her development of a private "shorthand of her own, which no one else could read, and although she has taken notes obsessively, daily, for years, of everything that she has considered to be of interest—the children's ailments, what their teachers said, other conversations, trips, readings, letters received, expenditures, sermons, lectures, outings, visits—most of them, unfortunately, have been in that code, in which her secrets are safe" (UO, 214). That detail organizes all the others around it because the real subject when he tells what he *does* know of his mother's life is what he does *not* know. "Beyond the day by day aspect of her existence, which she made over to us consciously, proudly, without fail—though not without moments of resentment—there was always a trackless, twilit, secret country open to no one. Not a dreamland or a cherished mystery into which she retired. It has always been right there with her, like her shadow, whatever she has been doing or saying" (UO, 218).

Her death becomes another instance of his lack of knowledge: "I did not know, of course, that by the time the words, and the picture of the monastery [on the postcard from Greece], with an arrow pointing to a window on the top floor, entered the white door of the farmhouse in Pennsylvania, my mother would be dead" (UO, 226). But his lack of knowledge was something she had cultivated. In spite of their having been able since Merwin's father's death "to speak more frankly than before" (UO, 204), they had "not really got very far" toward intimate communication. "She has been so secret, and I have grown up in the habit of being so reticent with her, that it cannot be easy now to find what we want to say to each other. And as I think of how little we have been able to tell each other of our lives so far, I realize how little I know of her, and how hard it is for either of us to follow the same subject for long in talking with each other, and even to pay sustained attention to what the other is saying" (UO, 204).

Even what Merwin knows about his mother is what he does not know. "Once she told me that there was a moment when she might have left my father," but Merwin apparently can only speculate on when that moment was. Similarly, even though he knows that the death of her first son, Hanson, only a few minutes after his birth, marks the boundary between "her legendary self" and "history," Merwin knows equally little about both sides of the boundary and refers to Hanson as one "Born into death like a message in a bottle" but laments that "The tide / Keeps coming in empty on the only shore" (MT, 28).

The mysteriousness of Merwin's mother extends beyond what she will not tell him. When he writes of her death in a poem, "Immortelles" (T, 89), he tells of "those flowers / fashioned of wire and some / kind of beads maybe glass" that had stood in a vase "motionless / on the polished water of / a small table" during his childhood. Here she gives him the information about which he is curious:

> what mattered about them
>
> as my mother had told me
> when I was old enough to understand
> was that they
> were not real they needed no water
> they would never change they would
> always be the same as they
> were while I stood watching. (T, 90)

That information, though, turns out to be unreliable. The irony of the poem is that the flowers were not always the same. At some point they were broken, and then were thrown out, so that they were even less permanent than the life whose transitoriness he is lamenting in the poem. Even her revelations turn out to be secrets or mysteries.

As was the case in "Tomatoes" and "Mary," in "La Pia" the crucial detail highlights one of the preoccupations that permeates

Merwin's work. In this case, it is the importance of mystery, the value of the unknown. His mother "was the unquestioned manifestation of the coherence of the world" (UO, 217), even though he knew so little about her, and one of the constant themes of his work has been the unifying, ordering presence of the unknown or the unknowable.

The first section of *Opening the Hand* continues the attempt, begun in *Unframed Originals,* to confront his feelings toward his parents. In the early poems in the sequence, like "The Oars" and "Sunset Water," the son's resentment of the father and his attempts at self-justification are clear. In "The Oars," the father's "passivity, his timidity in not leaving the shore, his mere waiting for the time to be up contrast sharply with the son's history, both in life and in poems, of setting out, journeying, taking risks."[20] In contrast to Merwin himself, whose personae in the poems have undertaken Odyssean wanderings, leaving behind the strictures of custom, the father here is portrayed as paralyzed. Unlike John Otto, unlike Noah's Raven, Merwin's father "sat in a rowboat / with its end on the bank below the house / holding onto the oars while the trains roared past" (OH, 4). Similarly, in "Sunset Water," although the father "seems pale and timid, and clearly out of his element, the son is at home in the water. He rides its rhythms, and accepts and values both the newness and the beauty of the scene."[21] Water was the primary venue for travel in his father's time: cities were built and commercial transport was conducted primarily along rivers, and travel between continents was by ship. In the son's time cities have come to be built primarily along roads, trains and trucks have assumed the largest portion of commercial transport, and travel between continents is typically by airplane, yet it is he who rocks "in smooth waves near the edge of the sea" (OH, 5), not only "at home" in the water but at one with it as "one by one the red waves out of themselves reach through me."

The resentment and self-assertion soften as the sequence of poems progresses. "Strawberries" recounts two premonitory experiences, one an observation and the other a dream, related to the father's death. While the narrator is outdoors "hoeing the sand of a small vegetable plot / for my mother" (OH, 7), he observes two farm wagons, one "going into the valley / carrying a casket" and the other "coming out of the valley" carrying "a high load / of two kinds of berries one of them strawberries." That night he "dreamed of things wrong in the house," including "an insect of a kind I had seen him kill / climbing around the walls of his bathroom." His mother's first words to him the next morning confirm the observation and the dream. Like the premonition in "The Waving of a Hand," the poem immediately preceding it, the premonitions in "Strawberries" are given without inflection, so they mimic the father's guardedness and also suggest that peculiar stage of grief in which the only feeling is numbness. The barely repressed anger of "The Oars," though, has disappeared.

In "The Houses" the dissonance that caused the anger is present, but the anger itself has been replaced by self-doubt. In this poem, "the son" recalls two different occasions on which he saw houses that "the father" said did not exist. In the first case, the two go to the site together, but there is no house; in the second, the disagreement ends with the father's denying the existence of the house the son believes he saw. The son "stops telling what he has seen" (OH, 14), although after the father's death he returns to both sites and sees both houses again. The difference between the father's point of view and the son's is portrayed as irreconcilable, but the father's authority induces the son to experience the difference as reason for self-doubt. He can verify his own experience for himself, but not in a way that will verify it for the father.

These earlier poems all build toward "Apparitions," one of the poems that attends to "the hand" of the book's title. "The dream images of the father in 'The Oars' and 'Sunset Water,' the psychic presentiments of his death in 'The Waving of a Hand' and 'Strawberries,' the play of imagination and memory of 'Sun and Rain' and 'The Houses' culminate in 'Apparitions.' Simply 'opening the hand' reminds the poet of the past's uncanny persistence in the present—of his bodily inheritance of a familial likeness."[22] "Apparitions" contains all the elements that appear separately in the other poems. In dream images the poet sees his parents' hands: "I will be looking down not from a window / and once more catch a glimpse of them hovering / above a whiteness like paper and much nearer than I would have thought" (OH, 15). The psychic presentiments of death are now presentiments of his own death. He remembers that he has not played the piano "for as long as their age" (OH, 16) and as he "feels mistakes approach" he recognizes what the hands became. In a play of imagination and memory, he envisions precisely recollected details about the hands as if the hands were actually present. He waits "for the smell of parsley and almonds" to "float to me from the polished translucent skin" (OH, 15). That play of imagination and memory culminates in the hands' absence:

> but as I recognize those hands they are gone
> and that is what they are as well as what they became
> without belief I still watch them wave to no one but me
> across one last room and from one receding car
> it is six years now since they touched anything
> and whatever they can be said to have held at all
> spreads in widening rings over the rimless surface[.]
> (OH, 16)

His own hands "that wash my face and tie my shoestrings / and have both sides and a day around them" are the only remnants of his parents' hands. Knowing "they are nobody's children" enforces recognition that he is his family now.

That in his works having to do with family history "reticence was one of the main things I was writing about," and that his "was a very reticent family" (RM, 326), makes "Yesterday" an important poem.[23] There he accepts some of the responsibility for that reticence rather than blaming it almost entirely on his parents as in the previous poems and memoirs. Itself reticent, "Yesterday" begins with "my friend" (and thereby makes use of the custom of talking about "a close friend of mine" when broaching difficult subjects) and then intentionally obscures the distinction between the friend and the "I." The first line says both that my friend blames himself for being a bad son and that my friend blames me for being a bad son, producing an ambiguity Merwin sustains throughout the poem. The son visits the father, but their apparently long-standing reticence asserts itself. The father catches the son looking at his watch and says "maybe / you have important work you are doing / or maybe you should be seeing / somebody I don't want to keep you" (OH, 21), to which the son replies that "it was so / and I got up and left him then," even though "there was nowhere I had to go / and nothing I had to do." Even if he learned it from his father, and even if it remains strong enough to necessitate only an indirect admission, the narrator clearly recognizes his own complicity in the reticence that marred his relationship with both parents. His awareness of that guilt brings about a reconciliation of sorts that leads the later family poems in *The Rain in the Trees, Travels,* and *The Vixen* to present more sympathetic portraits of his parents.

CHAPTER EIGHT

Hawaii

Hawaii has become "the last place" for Merwin, since apparently he plans to reside there until his death, and for humanity, symbolizing the last chance for humans to learn to live within the limits of the natural order instead of self-destructively attempting to overcome nature by manipulation, possession, and control. Hawaii fulfills Merwin's tragic vision by providing a haven where he can seek reconciliation with the forces that have shaped his earlier conflicts.

The facts underlying Merwin's symbolic treatment of Hawaii as "the last place" are straightforward. Its location, "more than 2,000 miles from the nearest continental land mass," makes Hawaii "the most geographically isolated place in the world."[1] Originally volcanic, the islands were populated initially by "a few hundred castaway species," brought "by winds and tides," that eventually "blossomed into at least 8,800 endemic plants and animals."[2] Around 400 A.D. the first humans arrived in Hawaii from Polynesia, bringing with them non-native plants and animals. The hunting and cultivation practiced by these first human settlers caused the extinction of at least 35 species of birds, including several species of flightless birds that made particularly easy prey.

When the English explorer James Cook arrived in 1778, the twin processes of importing alien species and extinguishing endemic species quickened, and now Hawaii stands out as "the endangered species capital of the nation." Although Hawaii's islands represent just two-tenths of one percent of total U.S. land area, three-quarters of the nation's extinct plants and birds once lived only there. Isolated islands are "more vulnerable to ecological invasion than any other landmasses": the Hawaiian islands are to the earth's ecosystem what the canary is to the mine.

Some of Merwin's recent essays about Hawaii provide an illuminating context in which to read the Hawaii poems in *Opening the Hand* (1983), *Travels* (1993), and especially *The Rain in the Trees* (1988). His 1989 essay "The Sacred Bones of Maui" narrates a specific conflict between a real-estate developer and native Hawaiians. The developer, Colin Cameron, planned to build a 450-room beachfront hotel for the Ritz-Carlton chain on a sand dune at Honokahua on Maui. But the dune was an ancient burial site that held the remains of over 900 burials, all of which "dated from long before European contact in the late 18th century." Some were more than 1,000 years old.[3]

The issue raised by the conflict over the Honokahua burial site / hotel site, according to Merwin, is whether what is native to a place, be it a native plant or human remains or a group of living humans, ought to be treated reverently or as an object for study or purchase or use. That issue pervades the series of "Questions to Tourists Stopped by a Pineapple Field" in *Opening the Hand:*

how do you like   these pineapple fields
have you ever seen   pineapple fields before
do you know whether pineapple   is native to the islands
do you know whether the natives   ate pineapple
do you know whether the natives   grew pineapple

do you know how the land was acquired   to be turned into
      pineapple fields
do you know what is done to the land   to turn it into
      pineapple fields
do you know how many months   and how deeply they plow it
do you know what those machines do   are you impressed
do you know what is in those containers   are you interested[.]
(43)

This poem pointedly illustrates the tourists' complicity in
the process of exploitation that Jan Zwicky says "occurs when a
thing becomes identified with a particular role in 'the story of
(Western European) (human) progress'; roughly, when it becomes a commodity; when it is used in the absence of a perception of what it *is*."[4] Real attention to the questions in the poem, by
forcing the reader to see the pineapple—as well as the fields in
which it is grown and the laborers involved in harvesting it—as
what it is rather than merely as the sum of what it can do for
consumers, therefore pushes the reader away from what Zwicky
calls exploitation to what the protesters in the Honokahua incident call respect.

Humor pervades the poem, as when the narrator asks whether
the auditor's hometown is "a growth community" and whether
"you think there is a future in pineapple" (45). But the poem
clearly pushes the reader not only toward knowledge of the
pineapple, but of the islands themselves ("what have you seen in
the last three miles"), and even toward self-knowledge ("when you
look at things in rows how do you feel" [44]). In doing so, it fulfills
Merwin's ambition that a poem should be a means of discovery.

HAWAII

The conflict over the environment of the Hawaiian islands shows Merwin the destructiveness of the human economic and technological ambitions against which his poems have protested since *The Moving Target* and *The Lice.* In a pair of letters dated October 1989 and January 1990, addressed to the readers of *American Poetry Review,* Merwin details one instance of that destructiveness. On the big island of Hawaii, he writes, grows the "largest intact bit of lowland rain forest remaining in the Hawaiian islands," a forest called the Wao Kele O Puna, the only place on the islands where native birds have developed resistance to avian malaria, and a part of the "ceded land" dedicated to the use of native Hawaiians. But the state of Hawaii "swapped" another area, composed of non-native forest, for the Wao Kele O Puna, "without asking the consent of native Hawaiians," in order to pursue a plan to dig within the forest twenty geothermal wells.[5]

In the letters, Merwin condemns the rapacity of a money-driven technological society willing to sacrifice a unique ecosystem for lower fuel bills. That same condemnation infuses his poem "Chord." Merwin's comparison in the letters between the peaceful activities of the native Hawaiians and the destructive activities of the developers becomes in the poem a comparison between the spiritual/aesthetic activities of the British poet John Keats and the technological/economic activities of the traders of Keats's day who clear-cut the native forests of Hawaii for wood.

While Keats wrote they were cutting down the sandalwood
    forests
while he listened to the nightingales they heard their own axes
    echoing through the forests

while he sat in the walled garden on the hill outside the city
    they thought of their gardens dying far away on the
    mountain
while the sound of the words clawed at him they thought of
    their wives
while the tip of his pen travelled the iron they had coveted was
    hateful to them[.] (RT, 66)

The self-despising woodcutters are only a particular instance of a danger Merwin warns against in more general terms in an earlier poem: "while we sign our names / more of us / lets go // and will never answer" (WUA, 37). Certain forms of living result in what Marx calls alienation, or what Tennessee Ernie Ford calls (equivalently) owing one's soul "to the company store." The Bible of Merwin's childhood says, "For what is a man profited, if he shall gain the whole world, and lose his own soul?"

Unfortunately, human self-destructiveness, as Merwin understands it, is never exclusively *self*-destructiveness. Humanity is taking whole species, whole ecosystems down in its fall. "Chord" laments what Keats's contemporaries did to themselves: "while he felt his heart they were hungry and their faith was sick." But it also laments what they did to Hawaii: "while the song broke over him they were in a secret place and they were cutting it forever."

The final line of "Chord," "an age arrived when everything was explained in another language," indicates that more than the native flora and fauna of the islands is being devastated: the "native" Hawaiian culture, formed from Polynesians who immigrated around 400 A.D., is being lost as well. "The Hawaiian culture," Merwin says, "is under terrible menace. There are no Hawaiians who don't speak English and many Hawaiians who don't speak Hawaiian. Draw your own conclusions. The land has been taken away and the culture has been downgraded and kept in pockets on the islands."[6]

The destruction of the flora and fauna and of the Hawaiian culture are interrelated. "In *The Rain in the Trees*," Merwin says, "I'm talking very literally when I speak about the loss of language. I feel that the loss of language is a direct result of the loss of the natural world, and the loss of different cultures. The language referred to in the book has to do with all the actual language that has been lost as we move farther and farther away from the sources of speech."[7] The problem can be put in simple terms. Language is rooted in place and loses accuracy and effectiveness when transplanted. A clichéd example is the variety of words for snow available to an Eskimo, to whom snow matters more than it does to residents of temperate regions. To a person for whom a tree is a tree, it will not matter that the 'ohia grows nowhere else. One for whom a tree is either hardwood for furniture or softwood for pulp, who uses a tree "in the absence of a perception of what it *is,*" will not care that sandalwood is being replaced by pine. Respect for local culture and for local environment are interconnected in language.

This is why Mark Jarman says that in *The Rain in the Trees* Merwin locates original sin "in the ignorance of nature with which he was brought up."[8] Jarman cites "Native Trees" as his example:

> Neither my father nor my mother knew
> the names of the trees

> where I was born
> what is that
> I asked and my
> father and mother did not
> hear they did not look where I pointed[.] (RT, 6)

This particular version of original sin accounts for the urgency in "Witness": "I want to tell what the forests / were like," and to do so "I will have to speak / in a forgotten language" (RT, 65).

One of the most powerful expressions of the two-horned problem of destruction of environment and destruction of culture is "Losing a Language":

> A breath leaves the sentences and does not come back
> yet the old still remember something that they could not say
>
> but they know now that such things are no longer believed
> and the young have fewer words
>
> many of the things the words were about
> no longer exist
>
> the noun for standing in mist by a haunted tree
> the verb for I[.] (RT, 67)

Because the children have learned their language from "the new owners" rather than from their parents, they think "it is better to say everything differently // so that they can be admired some-where / farther and farther away // where nothing that is here is known." The children are alienated from their parents, who are "wrong and dark," and alienated from the islands, which suffer physically from the loss of language. This, Merwin says, "is what the words were made / to prophesy // here are the extinct feathers / here is the rain we saw" (67).

Merwin faces the same problem in the poems about Hawaii that arises in other poems: how to write a "political" or "ecological" poem without making it a mere tract. He solves the problem in *The Rain in the Trees* and *Travels* the same way as before: by myth and music. In the poems of his youth he frequently mythologizes himself as the wandering Odysseus; in these poems of his maturity, Hawaii takes the place of Ithaca, and his lovers become Penelope. The musical devices remain underground, where they have been since *The Moving Target,* but they are present still. Even so short a poem as "The Inevitable Lightness" has frequent internal rhyme (fly, rises, dying, sky) and alliteration (roads, rises; dissolve, dying; scars, sky). Both myth and music are more muted in Merwin's maturity, but they remain important elements of his work.

Merwin sees Hawaii as an illustration of the conceptual errors that underlie the ecological destructiveness at which he thinks America excels. People often display incredulity on learning that he has chosen to live in Hawaii; he ascribes their shock to

the image broadcast with increasing effect in the course of this century by the tourist business: the poster world of beaches, sunsets, brown-skinned beauties wearing non-Hawaiian flowers, and so on. It certainly would be surpris-

ing to be told that someone from the real world of air-
conditioning, commuting, pollution, and debts had gone to
live there. But long before that counterfeit image became
current, a particularly European and American view of
things set civilization, science, industry, cities, virtue,
God, cleanliness, and reality on one side, and primitivism,
idleness, heathenism, ignorance, sensuality, iniquity, error, and unreality on the other. The belief system that
encouraged such a division was a self-serving, deadly
credo, and it has not gone away or grown less toxic.[9]

People do not understand his decision to live in Hawaii, he thinks,
because they have accepted the same mistaken belief system that
results in large-scale ecological destruction. He attempts to
counteract ecological damage by telling what he believes is the
truth, showing a "real" Hawaii instead of the Hawaii feigned by
business interests.

One way to tell a truth hidden by the counterfeit image is to
change scale. By focusing on something smaller than the sweep-
ing vistas of tourist brochures, "Empty Water" discovers what the
counterfeit images cover up. Merwin describes not the view
across the clouds from the rim of Haleakala or the endless sands
at Waikiki, but "the toad / who came all summer / to the limestone
water basin" (RT, 25). Seeing the toad allows him to consider the
Christmasberry tree under which the basin is located and to
narrate the tree's history. It was "imported in 1912 / from Brazil
for decoration" and grew from "a weed on a mule track / on a
losing / pineapple plantation" into "an old tree in a line / of old
trees" that most people no longer recognize as non-indigenous.

HAWAII

The obvious irony in Merwin's concern for preservation of native plants, animals, and humans is that Merwin himself is new to Hawaii. Like the developers who cut down the sandalwood forests in Keats's time and who build hotels in our own, Merwin claims to own a portion of Hawaii as his property. He resolves the paradox for himself by an approach like that of John F. Kennedy in his "Ich bin ein Berliner" speech, claiming that force of empathy forges a new identity. Thus the title of "Native" implies both that the speaker is tending plants that are native and that the speaker is himself native. His attention to native history generates not just sympathy but identity:

> I go down the slope
> where mules I never saw
> plowed in the sun and died
> while I was in school
>
> they were beaten to go
> straight up the hill
> so that in three years the rain
> had washed all the topsoil
>
> out past sea cliffs
> and frigate birds
> only a few years
> after the forests were gone[.] (RT, 63)

Since knowing history still fails to transform one into a native, he longs to reverse that history, to salve the wound history has exposed, so he goes past the non-indigenous mango tree to find "the small native / plants in their plastic pots" that he will plant. He recognizes the irony, noting that their names are written in Latin, but insists on his identification with what is native: the "seeds from destroyed valleys" are under "ohia trees / filled with red flowers red birds," in "the shade of leaves I have put there."

Merwin gives many reasons for living on an island, not least of which is his view that the global center of culture has shifted in this century from one ocean to another. "I grew up with the assumption that the center of human venture was the American Northeast and its European motherland. But it is the civilizations circling the Pacific, as well as Latin America, that I turn to increasingly."[10] He gives, in fact, an even more specific location for the center of culture: "The Pacific to me historically is now the focus of history. For years for me it was New York; but now it really seems to be somewhere in the Pacific, probably on the uninhabited island of Kahoolawe, which the Navy is bombing."[11] But his central explanation for living in Hawaii is a variation on John Donne's famous assertion that "no man is an island." Perhaps no one *is* an island, but in Merwin's view everyone lives on one. "Things here are on a scale that seems human. And living on an island, in the country, in our time, is a constant reminder of the finite condition of the natural world, and of what, from a narrow point of view, are commonly referred to as 'resources.' There is only so much coast, so much of anything. It is easy to be aware that everyone lives on an island."[12] Awareness that one lives on an island, Merwin thinks, heightens one's moral, aesthetic, and ecological sensitivity, for the same reason that asking what supplies a person would take to a desert island exposes what is truly valuable.

Merwin has no delusions about the magnitude of his actions or the effect of his writings. He knows that a government centered thousands of miles away will remain unresponsive to the unique needs of the Hawaiian islands and its inhabitants, especially given the economic motivations of that government. "Despite the speeches and the presence of tourists and the military," Merwin says, "despite the local maneuvers of multinational corporations based heaven knows where, the mainland and the Federal government seem, most of the time, remote and unreal," adding that "the Federal government's directives regarding Hawaii sometimes add to the sense of remoteness."[13] One ill-conceived government directive is a plan that "proposes spraying all the Hawaiian Islands, over a period of six years, with six poisons, three of them organophosphates, several of them suspected carcinogens and mutagens" (236). The purpose of the plan is to rid the islands of three species of fruit fly, even though Hawaii already uses ten times as much poison per square mile, and three times as much per capita, as any other state (237).

Merwin is not without hope for the islands, though. In spite of the destruction wrought on them, the ravines for which Haiku, the district in which Merwin lives, is named "are a direct link with the island's past (every watercourse on the coast has not only its Hawaiian name but its own legends), with its botanical and geological origins, its native self."[14] And the character of the islands retains its spellbinding effect in spite of the activities of governments and developers. "A love of the tropics is bound to be physical, influenced by an unfathomable response to the flood of sunlight, the massive rains, the air itself. For me the attraction was part of a continuing gravitation toward the neighborhood of trees and mountains, rain forests, dry forests, mountain ridges, and sea cliffs."[15] Some aspects of the islands, such as the volcanic terrain and the isolated location, cannot be changed by even the most rapacious humans.

The poems themselves are hopeful, also, as in "Place," which begins "On the last day of the world / I would want to plant a tree" (RT, 64). The prominence of the last day of the world reminds one of Merwin's earlier apocalyptic poems, especially those in *The Moving Target* and *The Lice,* but the speaker's desire to plant a tree on that day points out the difference between Merwin's apocalypse then and now. In the earlier apocalyptic poems, the imminent disaster judges our current actions (which have made it inevitable) and destroys any possibility of present happiness. The night and the shadow of the last one already have put on the same head and said Now. They are prepared to swallow our shadows. Already we are following the gray whale to The End. In "Place," though, the present is wholly independent of the future. The speaker is not planting the tree for its fruit. The present is independent of the future even without impending doom: "the tree that bears the fruit / is not the one that was planted." That the last day of the world is already on its way, regardless of the speaker's actions, frees him from responsibility. He chooses to plant a tree because the tree has long functioned for Merwin synecdochically, standing for the whole of nature. In *The Lice,* for instance, "The Last One" is a tree. Planting a tree on the last day of the world affirms the intrinsic worth of nature. This poem is Merwin's answer to the slumber-party question, "What would you do if you knew you only had one day to live?," intensified by giving everything only one day to live.

Both sides in the ecological debate typically frame their positions in terms of the consequences for humans. We should save the habitat of the spotted owl because humans suffer from the loss of wilderness and from diminished biodiversity, says one side; we should let the spotted owl fend for itself because we need the wood and the jobs, says the other. But Merwin frames his ecological statement without reference to consequences. Humans should achieve ecological harmony with the natural environment because of its intrinsic worth.

> I want the tree that stands
> in the earth for the first time
>
> with the sun already
> going down
>
> and the water
> touching its roots
>
> in the earth full of the dead
> and the clouds passing
>
> one by one
> over its leaves[.] (RT, 64)

That intrinsic value, Merwin appears to believe, will win out over our attempts to exploit the environment. In "Rain at Night," the central poem of *The Rain in the Trees,* the end is invoked again, this time not by imagining the last day of the world but by setting the poem in December, the last month of the year, and describing the actions of humans who saw nature exclusively as a source of selfish benefit: "after an age of leaves and feathers / someone dead / thought of this mountain as money / and cut the trees." The line breaks isolate the phrase "someone dead," drawing attention to the double entendre: the cutting is initiated by someone who is now dead (since the cutting occurred many years ago), but more importantly the person who initiated the cutting was already "dead" then, in virtue of his lack of connection with nature. The speaker expresses pain and disbelief at the cutting:

> it is hard to say it
> but the cut the sacred 'ohias then
> the sacred koas then
> the sandalwood and the halas
> holding aloft their green fires[.] (RT, 26)

This expression of pain exemplifies the same attitude of respect toward the trees that the Hawaiian protesters asked for toward their ancestors in the Honokahua incident. It "does not bring back the fields and farmland or the sweet smell of sandalwood forests, nor make recompense to the lives lost to history. It will not stop wars or stay death. Merwin, for all his acute awareness of loss, writes not to alter the world but to honor it."[16]

The sandalwood and the 'ohias were cut down just like "The Last One" in *The Lice,* but in that poem revenge for the destruction followed. By the time of "Rain at Night," Merwin sees resilience. Instead of *getting* back, the trees *come* back. Merwin is no less aware in 1988 of wholesale ecological destruction than he was in 1967, but the later Merwin musters hope. He finds in the Hawaiian flora and fauna the same insistence articulated by one of the proverbs he had translated years before: "Nations die / rivers go on / mountains / go on."[17] Even after use, the trees' intrinsic value remains, and even after woodcutters die, koas go on, halas go on.

> the trees have risen one more time
> and the night wind makes them sound
> like the sea that is yet unknown
> the black clouds race over the moon
> the rain is falling on the last place[.] (RT, 26)

CHAPTER NINE

France

In a 1984 interview, Merwin describes an as-yet-unpublished prose book about Hawaii as "a gathering together of almost all of my interests—interest in nonliterate peoples, in their and our relation to the earth, to the primal sources of things, our relation to the natural world, our relation to and necessary opposition to the overweening authority of institutions and institutionalized greed, the destruction of the earth for abstract and greedy reasons" (RM, 349). But that description would fit any of the books from *Opening the Hand* on: all of Merwin's concerns (myth, apocalypse, ecology, society, love, family) resolve themselves into a concern for *place*. In keeping with the increasing reliance on reminiscence characteristic of age, his two most recent books, *The Lost Upland* and *The Vixen,* focus on a recollected place, southwest France, where Merwin once lived, the passing of whose provincial culture he laments as he had lamented in *The Carrier of Ladders* the elimination of the native culture of continental America and in *The Rain in the Trees* the loss of native Hawaiian culture.

What Ed Folsom says of Merwin's home in Hawaii can also be said of his home in France. "The Thoreauvian attention to day-to-day details of living in the natural world, his penetrating attachment to the place he lives his life in, is part of what marks Merwin's poetry from *The Compass Flower* on. His home in Hawaii, which he built, works for him much like the Walden cabin did for Thoreau; it is an extension of himself, a modest exfoliation of his needs, a center from which he can observe his environment, measure the quality of the land and of his life, remain somewhat isolated and aloof from human society (though close enough so he can visit)."[1] Once Hawaii teaches him that place resolves the moral and ecological problems that preoccupy him, Merwin is prepared to see that he had intuited that resolution in France, and acknowledging that intuition prepares the way for the stories in *The Lost Upland* and the poems in *The Vixen.* "The last place" teaches him that it was never the only place.[2]

"Thoreauvian attention" pervades *The Lost Upland* and *The Vixen,* both of which savor detail. Merwin minutely describes details of landscape and personality that would have seemed distracting to the younger mythologizing poet. In "Present," the narrator recounts an elderly woman's gift of a bag of plums. This simple poem derives its force from the accretion of detail. We are told that mirabelle plums, the type she brought, are "not so big as all the others / but they are more delicate for those acquainted with them" (V, 21). We are told the size of the woman's house and of her garden, what she grows in her garden and when, and even why she grew what she did: "it was a cold garden / facing north so it was slow in spring better for summer." We watch as "a snow of plum blossoms" is "swept across the valley in the morning sunlight." And we learn about the woman herself: "when she bent in her garden / she disappeared in the rows it took her a long time / to stand up to turn around to let herself through / the gate to walk to do anything." When the narrator at the end recounts the actual occasion of the gift, the details make a picture complete enough to explain the significance not only of the gift but of the woman's life.

late one day that summer she appeared at the wall
    carrying a brown paper bag wet at the bottom
the mirabelles she whispered but she would not come in
    we sat on the wall and opened the bag look she said
how you can see through them and each of us held up
    a small golden plum filled with the summer evening[.]

The litany of detail, though, might lead the reader to miss the forest for the trees, as does even so well-trained and attentive a reader as Sven Birkerts. Comparing *The Lost Upland* to *Unframed Originals* (which he describes as the best of Merwin's books), Birkerts says,

> *The Lost Upland* invokes a different subject [than does *Unframed Originals*] and uses a grown-up narrator as its narrative filter. But we know, somehow, that no matter how carefully the author scrutinizes his neighbors and the terrain, the otherness will never dissolve. Nor is there as much at stake as there is in the family reconnaissance. This is more purely writing, prose fulfilling an anthropological function. The result is that, for all its beauty and delicacy, the book is curiously static. It ends up being the preservation of a distance rather than a more determined effort to breach it.[3]

No evaluation of *The Lost Upland* could be more mistaken. Much *more* is at stake here than in the family recollections of *Unframed Originals.* There Merwin traces his origins to understand himself and analyzes his parents in order to grieve for them fully. That Merwin himself is at stake might seem to lend credence to Birkerts's evaluation. But in *The Lost Upland* a whole culture, and by extension all of humankind, is at stake. Merwin laments the loss of the provincial culture of the southwestern French countryside for the same reasons an ecologist mourns a species that has become extinct: the worst problem is not the loss per se, but what it betokens. No human being noticed when the last ivory-billed woodpecker died: the extinction of the species was confirmed only after many years went by without a sighting. Yet, the extinction of the species is significant because it adds to the ever-growing list of animal species eliminated by the effects of humans on the environment and warns that we humans are moving in the direction of our own extinction.

Similarly, very few people, even among the French themselves, will notice when the local culture of the region where Merwin lived is fully assimilated into the mass culture of Europe. Yet that loss warns of something larger. Humanity is intent on expanding across the planet to control nature, and a few woodpeckers is a small price to pay; the mass culture of acquisitive capitalism is intent on expanding across cultures to control the global economy, and a few backward shepherds and vintners is a small price to pay. But the latter, like the former, signals unwitting self-destruction.

Merwin's objection to mass culture resembles British poet William Blake's critique of religion in "The Marriage of Heaven and Hell." Blake says, "The ancient Poets animated all sensible objects with Gods or Geniuses, calling them by the names and adorning them with the properties of woods, rivers, mountains, lakes, cities, nations, and whatever their enlarged & numerous senses could perceive. And particularly they studied the genius of each city & country, placing it under its mental deity." But then priests "enslav'd the vulgar by attempting to realize or abstract the mental deities from their objects," with the result that "men forgot that All deities reside in the human breast."[4] Mass religion, in contrast to local religion, says Blake, is inanimate. Merwin's view of culture is identical: local culture is animate, mass culture is inanimate. Merwin makes this comparison most directly through his depictions of architecture in "Foie Gras," where he says that local buildings, having developed along with the character of the inhabitants, attained their distinctive form in the Middle Ages (LU, 38). The houses, for instance, have a unique character: "on the uplands the oldest roofs had been built of slabs of limestone and were pitched high because of the weight and the angle at which the stones lay. Later they had been roofed with flat tiles hooked to lathes of split chestnut, but the lower rows along the eaves were often still formed of the original stone" (LU, 40). The architecture derived from the particular character of the materials that the place provided. In contrast, when M. and Mme. Bargues modernize the old building to make their supermarket, they sever its connection with its place. "The renovations tore out the severe classical doorway, near the corner, removed as much of the ground-floor façade as was structurally feasible and replaced it with sheets of glass, gutted the interior completely, covered the walls and the floor with bright, hard synthetic materials, filled it with fluorescent lights and islands of shelves, and lined the sides with refrigerated cases and freezers with glass doors" (LU, 52). The houses on the upland came from the upland; they belong to the upland. The supermarket came from Paris and could go anywhere.

Thoreauvian attention to detail characterizes Merwin's most
recent work, but the scene in "Shepherds" in which M. Vert and
the narrator build a funeral pyre for the dead sheep well illustrates
other transformations from Merwin's earliest to his most mature
work. The episode has an obvious predecessor in the funeral of
Patroclus from *The Iliad,* and Merwin emphasizes the connection. In *The Iliad,* Agamemnon orders a funeral pyre built for
Patroclus:

> These then
> went out and in their hands carried axes to cut wood
> and ropes firmly woven, and their mules went on ahead of them.
> They went many ways, uphill, downhill, sidehill and slantwise;
> but when they came to the spurs of Ida with all her well springs,
> they set to hewing with the thin edge of bronze and leaning
> their weight to the strokes on towering-leafed oak trees that
>   toppled
> with huge crashing; then the Achaians splitting the timbers
> fastened them to the mules and these with their feet tore up
> the ground as they pulled through the dense undergrowth . . .[5]

In "Shepherds" M. Vert orders a similar pyre built for the sheep.
Here the narrator instead of the soldiers builds the pyre, but it is
still a monumental pyre (as tall as the narrator himself) and it is
still of oak. "M. Vert came back and asked me whether I would
mind making a pile of brush in the near end of the upper pasture,
to burn the bodies. There where I'd come to get the firewood the
night before. . . . I went up and started, carefully laying the brush
of the oaks that I had watched in their lifetime from the window

at the other end of the pasture, building a pyre some fifteen feet across, as the sun rose" (LU, 145).

In *The Iliad,* Achilles drags Hector's corpse behind his chariot; in "Shepherds" sheep rather than a soldier are dragged, the dragging is done by a tractor instead of horses, and it is not done with malicious intent toward the corpses, but it *is* still done from grief and anger, and the resemblance is clear enough.

> M. Vert took the tractor down into the bottom of the lower pasture and turned it so that its back was to the wide gap in the fence. Out in the woods he tied the legs of dead sheep, that were still attached to bodies, together with twine from the bales of straw, and then hauled them to the end of a wire towing cable hooked to the tractor.
>
> . . . .
> He made a pile of ten of them at the end of the cable, and tied them with wire and started up the tractor. The wire tightened and rose in the air and the pile of bodies began to move. It slid over the wet ground leaving a track in the mud and across stones, bits of wool, blood, the heads catching as they went on brambles and stumps. (LU, 145)

This allusion to Achilles serves a very different purpose from Merwin's earlier uses of myth, which typically serve to distance us from the "merely" personal. Now the use of myth instead of distancing us from the personal shows us its broader significance. Birkerts did not see that this story recounts a minor tragedy in the life of an obscure French shepherd in order to depict its universal implications. Achilles thought the whole world had suffered when Patroclus died, and Merwin thinks the whole world is suffering (without knowing it) when M. Vert's sheep are run over by a train.

The pyre episode differs both from Merwin's earlier uses of pre-given myths and from his earlier creation of his own myths. Compare the pyre episode to "Burning the Cat" from *Green with Beasts*. In both cases, the burning of the animals becomes emblematic of something larger, but here the difference is in the subtlety of the emblematization. In the early poem, the narrator's account of burning a dead cat states its conclusion baldly:

> . . . hours I fed
> That burning, till I was black and streaked with sweat;
> And poked it out then, with charred meat still clustering
> Thick around the bones. And buried it so
> As I should have done in the first place, for
> The earth is slow, but deep, and good for hiding;
> I would have used it if I had understood
> How nine lives can vanish in one flash of a dog's jaws,
> A car or copperhead, and yet how one small
> Death, however reckoned, is hard to dispose of. (FF, 167–68)

In the story, though, Merwin follows Wittgenstein's advice: "Anything your reader can do for himself leave to him."[6] Rather than *say,* in the pyre episode or anywhere else in the book, that the loss of a provincial culture is a tragedy for all humankind, he *shows* it in the inadvertent deaths of M. Vert's sheep on the train tracks no less than in the "chill smile" of Mme. Bargues behind the Formica counter of her new supermarket and in Blackbird's inability to find anyone who appreciates the difference between handcrafted and mass-produced wines enough to take over his business after his death.

The loss of the provincial culture of southwest France is tragic for humanity, according to Merwin, because local culture is absent from the mass culture fostered by capitalism, of which America is representative. Mass culture lacks connection to place. America was the perfect place for mass culture to develop since, as Robert Frost points out in his poem "The Gift Outright," Americans never have been connected to place: "Something we were withholding from our land of living."[7] The French, in contrast, *have* been connected to place, Merwin says. "I suppose it would be simpler to say that they have loved their place for generations, centuries; and know it, without having to make a fuss about it. Whereas, by comparison, we begin as a loveless people. Generation after generation having cared little for the place. Our fathers began by caring little enough about Europe so that they could leave it. We've used the place, wasted it. It has made us prodigal, restless" (RM, 187). The tragedy narrated in *The Lost Upland* is that our prodigality is infecting others.

In *The Moving Target* and *The Lice,* Merwin treated ecological and social problems prophetically. In *The Vixen* and *The Lost Upland,* he treats them elegiacally. His ecological statements in the earlier books had a tone of portent and conveyed the threat of ruin, as in "The Last One," where the last one strikes back, exacting its revenge on them "whom the birds despise," consuming all but "the lucky ones" (L, 10–12). In the two most recent books, the tone of lamentation conveys the reality of loss, as in the discussion of new mass agricultural techniques in "Shepherds."

A tractor-drawn plow enables a farmer to plow much more ground in much less time than does an animal-drawn plow. But the efficiency is gained at the cost of an inevitable loss: the walnut trees indigenous to the area. "Until the middle of the century," Merwin states, "in most parts of the *causse,* plowing had been done with cows. Not oxen, usually, but the same red, long-horned, notoriously self-willed cows that supplied the rich milk on the farms, and the milk-fed veal, and the beef" (LU, 92). Plowing with cows may be more difficult than it is with a tractable tractor, but it has an advantage. "When the cows were plowing a field near a tree, and the plow hit a root, the cows stopped. One freed the plow and one went on. When a plow drawn by a tractor hit a root it kept going and cut the root." And therein lies the loss: "One could not cut walnut roots with impunity. There were only two periods in the year when you could cut the limbs aboveground—a few weeks in the spring, after the hard frosts but before the sap began its main rise, and in the fall, after the sap went down and the leaves fell but before the real freeze. Cut them at any other time and the tree might bleed to death or be so weakened that it would never recover, or would freeze and crack, and bleed away later. And the roots should not be cut at all. The tree might bleed into the field, unseen" (LU, 92).

A similar problem holds for the new agribusiness shepherding methods, which damage the walnut trees—since sheep kept in barns do not fertilize the trees—and are cruel to the sheep themselves. The lambs at the sheep fair at Bordeaux, brought from the Netherlands or New Zealand, "were flung out from the stinking hot hold of the ship in which they had traveled for weeks. Picked up by a leg or a handful of wool and thrown into the upper story of a truck, which drove them for hours and hours to the new barn, where they were unloaded in the same way. And once they were inside they never saw the light of day again" (LU, 93). The sheep are taken out of a natural cycle and made part of a manufacturing cycle, with as little regard for their well-being as was paid to that of women and children working in factories at the beginning of the industrial revolution.[8]

There are direct effects on humans as well. Sheep pastured in the open fertilize the ground. In contrast, sheep kept in barns pollute the water. "Many thousands of sheep, over a period of months until they attained the desired weight, would eat, evacuate, and eventually bleed," and the waste "would have to be removed continuously. And for this, the developers maintained, they must have water. It must come in clean, which was not difficult along the valley with its small clear crayfish streams winding through woods," but "on the downstream side of the new barns the current would emerge full of the warm contents of bowels, bladders, and veins of lambs and sheep fattened on chemically souped-up feed" (LU, 94). This is not a prophetic foretelling of human destruction, but an expression of grief over current realities. The *causse* that once had its own aroma, rich with walnut and plum, wool and limestone, now reeks of fetid barns. The shepherds used to share their lambs with each other at slaughtering time. "Each family, they said, had had its own secret formula for feeding the lambs during the last weeks. Thyme and marjoram and carrot tops, and other things about which they remained mysterious. You could tell from the taste, then, which family had raised the lamb. But then, of course, they had eaten their own lamb, taking turns, one farm after another butchering and dividing it" (LU, 108). Now butchering one's own sheep is illegal; the lambs, raised in barns on packaged feed, have no distinctive flavor; and the meat is stored in freezers instead of being eaten fresh. The shepherds used to sing together, but now they do not sing at all (LU, 134).

Any expression of grief is grounded in memory, which "allows one to call from the past what matters, what has an essential relation to the self," which is "manifested as a desire for coherence and recurrence."[9] We speak of the loss of memory associated with Alzheimer's disease as a tragedy for a person and his or her family. We say, with grief, such statements as "He's not himself anymore," and we expect death to follow within only a few months to a few years after the onset of the disease. In *The Lost Upland* and *The Vixen,* Merwin is depicting the onset of a cultural Alzheimer's disease: now that the local culture of "the lost upland" is losing its memory, he thinks it is "not itself anymore," and he laments its imminent death.

One instance of this loss of cultural memory occurs in the conflict between Blackbird and his daughter Françoise over the sign in front of their hotel. They argue while they are having M. Milibou perform other renovations, including papering walls. Françoise is not satisfied: "she kept wanting something that would not have come out of M. Milibou's sample books, something superior. Her broodings settled on the hotel façade, and she concluded that it would be a good time to change the sign painted across the whole front of the building, the name 'Hotel Blackbird' on the frieze of vines and blackbirds" (LU, 223–24). But when she suggests changing the sign, Blackbird first misunderstands, thinking she means only "the painted placard that stood by the entrance during the summer" (LU, 224), and then rejects her idea as soon as he understands it. She wants to use modern letters in the name.

> "What kind of modern letters?"
> "You know what they are. Like—" She thrashed around vainly for an example.
> "I know what you mean," Robert said.
> "Yes." Matthew said, trying to be helpful. "Modern. You see it everywhere. Filling stations. TOTAL. Like that."
> "Even neon, maybe," she said.

She gets the workers to agree that they could make such a sign, but Blackbird dismisses the idea, for a reason best expressed by one of the workers: "'Oh, they are the sign of the place,' Robert said. 'Vines. Blackbirds.'" But Françoise, the representative of mass culture who has lost her connection to place, has also lost her cultural memory and complains that the vines' always having been there is no reason to keep them.

Merwin's portrayal of the elimination of cultural memory in France in *The Lost Upland* and *The Vixen* contains elements from his earlier portrayals of the loss of cultural memory elsewhere. For instance, "Forgotten Streams" echoes the concerns of "Losing a Language." In the earlier poem, he laments that the disappearance of a language also severs a relationship with the earth: a new language does not contain the words that developed in order to describe a particular place and tries instead to impose its own words on a place to which they are not suited. So "many of the things the words were about / no longer exist" (RT, 67). In

FRANCE

"Forgotten Streams," the landscape is France instead of Hawaii, but the idea that the disappearance of a language severs a relationship with the earth remains the same: "The names of unimportant streams have fallen / into oblivion the syllables have washed away" (V, 20) and with them has gone our connection to the land.

> no one any longer recalls the Vaurs and the Divat
> the stream Siou Sujou Suzou and every speaker
>   for whom those were the names they have all become
> the stream of Lherm we do not speak the same language
>   from one generation to another and we
> can tell little of places where we ourselves have lived
>   the whole of our lives and still less of neighborhoods
> where our parents were young[.]

Merwin is resigned to the inevitable ("something keeps going on without looking back"), but that does not prevent its being an occasion for grief, any more than the inevitability of his parents' deaths prevented their being occasions for grief.

But the poems in *The Vixen* also pick up even earlier themes. Merwin has long been preoccupied with the spiritual impermanence of physically solid things. As early as *The Moving Target,* he writes a poem in which "things" speak ironically. They announce that they are "better than friends" (MT, 12), that they are "the anchor of your future," that they "will give you interest on yourself as you deposit yourself" with them, and that they try to please their possessors. They conclude by imploring the reader to depend on them. He depicts the reverse side of the same theme in "From a Mammon Card" (MPC, 204), when he reminds "those who work, as they say, for a living" that "what they claim to own is perhaps all that remains of what they sold that many hours of their life for," challenging them to "try to imagine the hours coming again."

Merwin revisits that theme with a pair of poems in *The Vixen,* "Possessions" (V, 51) and "Legacies" (V, 52). The choice of words for the titles already indicates that these poems form a contrasting pair. Although the words have a range of meaning that allows their being used to denote a single referent, 'possession' connotes physical objects, while 'legacy' connotes something more abstract; 'possession' only implies the present moment, while 'legacy' implies a temporal continuity. In keeping with the titles, "Possessions" elicits a negative judgment about the spiritual impermanence of objects, and "Legacies" elicits a positive judgment about the relative permanence of insubstantial experiences.

"Possessions" narrates the acquisition and then the loss of wealth. The ancestors of "Madame la Vicomtesse" had acquired "vast estates such riches beyond estimation" by "marriage by death by purchase by reparation," and she "was heir to it all." However, she "found it poor in variety and after her marriage / was often away visiting family and so on / leaving the chateau in the keeping of her / father-in-law who was almost totally deaf," so predictably "the son of a laborer" broke in to the house through a window and stole all of her jewels. The poem concludes:

> it was these absences
> that were commemorated at the next family wedding

at which the Vicomtesse wore at her neck and wrists
pink ribbons in place of the jewels that had been hers
it was for the ribbons that she was remembered. (V, 51)

The only permanence or continuity available to her, despite her uncountable possessions, was precisely the absence of possessions. The paradox she presents is reminiscent of the epigraph to *The Lice:* what she owned she left behind, and only what was stolen was hers.

In contrast, Louis the carpenter owns little, but he knows what Madame la Vicomtesse did not: that possessing something is a trivial relationship to it. The carpenter takes his elder son and the narrator out to look at his walnut trees because he is beginning to feel his age. He takes them to "the land plowed in the autumn on the windswept / ridge those fields that had come down to him from his grandmother / who had lived beside them once." When they arrive at the trees Louis tells the other two

that when those walnut trees were planted
a few years back when his son was a child they had dug
down to the limestone and had tipped into each hole
half a cart load of wool waste left over from the carding
machine
there were finches blowing across the blue sky behind
the bare limbs as he talked and he touched the young trees
with their grafting scars still plain on the bark and their branches
formed of wool that had grown through a single summer and
come back to winter barns carrying the day's weather[.] (V, 52)

For Merwin, Louis embodies several positive values. He has a healthy relationship with the land, as shown not only by his growing the walnut trees but also by his participation in natural cycles: he returns the sheep's by-products to the earth, unlike the polluting farmers who raise their sheep in barns. He has a healthy relationship with his family, as shown not only by his involving his son in the task of planting the trees but also by his taking the son to see the results. He has a healthy cultural memory, as shown by his reminiscence about where his grandmother lived. In short, Louis possesses a sense of place, which he is shown as passing on to his son. The legacies of the walnut trees and all that surrounds them are, on Merwin's view, more valuable than all the land and jewels of the Vicomtesse.

"After Fires" links this familiar theme of spiritual vs. material possession with the broader theme of mass culture's destruction of local culture by depicting a house fire to which the community members rush. The sons of the woman whose house is burning try to find the iron safe containing her papers and money, but they find it too late: "there was nothing inside but a small drift of black snow" (V, 62).

No poem better captures the spirit of *The Vixen,* though, than "Passing" (V, 55), which employs the technique of accretion of detail as well as any poem in the book. Even Merwin's beloved Thoreau would be hard-pressed to match the precision of detail in this image:

a few surviving sparrows flew up ahead of me
    from gray splinters of grass hidden under the bitter
thymes and across the stony plain a flurry of sheep

was inching like a shadow they had the rain behind them
they were stopping to nose the scattered tufts while two silent
dogs kept moving them on and two boys with blankets
on their shoulders would bend one at a time to pick up
a stone and throw it to show the dogs where to close in
on the straggling flock the far side of it already
swallowed up in the mist[.] (V, 55)

This poem accomplishes what *The Vixen* aims for as a volume. Its portrayal of local culture summarizes the direction of Merwin's career by resolving his concerns with ecology, family, society, and so on into a single experience tied to place. It expresses a wish that might be applied to any of Merwin's books: "I stood there as they edged on and I wanted to call / to them as they were going I stood still wanting / to call out something at least before they had disappeared."

Introduction—Merwin's Career

1. "Merwin, W(illiam) S(tanley)," *Current Biography* 49:5 (May 1988): 384.

2. "I started writing hymns for my father almost as soon as I could write at all" (RM, 301).

3. Peter Davison, "In Search of Ararat: W. S. Merwin, 1956–1959," in *The Fading Smile: Poets in Boston, 1955–1960 from Robert Frost to Robert Lowell to Sylvia Plath* (New York: Alfred A. Knopf, 1994), 92. On this point, accounts of Merwin's life are not consistent. Cheri Davis, for instance, says that Merwin's first marriage was to Diana Whalley and occurred in 1954.

4. Lucy Frost, "The Poetry of W. S. Merwin: An Introductory Note," *Meanjin* 30 (1971): 294–96.

5. Davison, 92–93.

6. Merwin, "The Wake of the Blackfish," 302–3. Merwin's own description of the change in his personal life is echoed by Stephen Stepanchev's description of the change in Merwin's poetry: "There is a point in the career of a poet when he is no longer excited by his own manner; he must change for the sake of his survival as a poet, for the sake of his sense of the truth of things. This seems to have happened to Merwin. At any rate, the style of *The Moving Target* (1963) could not have been predicted on the basis of the four earlier books" ("W. S. Merwin," 118).

7. Merwin, "The Wake of the Blackfish," 303. The story of the inheritance and how he came to buy the farmhouse is recounted in "Hotel" in *Unframed Originals.*

8. Dinitia Smith, "A Poet of Their Own," *New York Times Magazine* (February 19, 1995): 41.

Chapter 1—Guides

1. Regarding his reputation for difficulty, Merwin himself expresses surprise. "For years I thought that I was writing more and more simply and directly," he says, "and people kept saying the poems were getting more and more difficult, opaque, harder to read" (RM, 343). Regarding the use of Merwin's own comments on poetry, I should clarify that they should be used only as a starting point, not as a set of limiting boundaries: good poetry generates more meaning than its author puts into it.

2. "Was That a Real Poem or Did You Just Make It Up Yourself?," in *The Collected Essays of Robert Creeley* (Berkeley: University of California Press, 1989), 576.

3. In other words, Merwin is asserting that the question of whether metrical verse or free verse is better for making poems is a "false dilemma," a logical fallacy that gives two choices as if they were the only available choices, when in fact they are not.

4. *Meno* 80d, in *The Collected Dialogues of Plato,* ed. Edith Hamilton and Huntington Cairns (Princeton: Princeton University Press, 1961), 363.

5. Merwin's answer is not peculiar to poetry. For instance, Michael Polanyi, in *Personal Knowledge: Towards a Post-Critical Philosophy* (Chicago: University of Chicago Press, 1958), gives a nearly identical answer to the same question in regard to scientific knowledge. To the question "How can we concentrate our attention on something we don't know?," Polanyi replies that we look at "the manner in which [the] known particulars hang together" (127–28), which is revelatory because form and content are one.

6. Job 1:1. I am, of course, in no position to assess the morality of Merwin's life.

7. Oliver Wendell Holmes, "The Chambered Nautilus."

8. *Grounding for the Metaphysics of Morals,* trans. James W. Ellington (Indianapolis: Hackett, 1981), 36.

9. *The Antichrist,* in *The Portable Nietzsche,* ed. and trans. Walter Kaufmann (New York: Viking, 1968), 577.

10. *The Gospel of Mark* 16:15.

11. *Republic* 520a–d, in *The Collected Dialogues,* 752.

12. *A Mask for Janus,* in *The First Four Books of Poems,* 23. My citations of the first four books will use the pagination not of the individual volumes but of the now more widely available *The First Four Books.*

13. Roberto Calasso, *The Marriage of Cadmus and Harmony,* trans. Tim Parks (New York: Alfred A. Knopf, 1993), 93.

14. *W. S. Merwin,* 62.

15. In Michael Clifton, "W. S. Merwin: An Interview," 17–22.

16. In Richard Jackson, "Unnaming the Myths," 51.

17. Quoted in Frank MacShane, "A Portrait of W. S. Merwin," 12.

18. W. H. Auden, "In Memory of W. B. Yeats," in *Collected Poems,* ed. Edward Mendelson (New York: Random House, 1976), 197.

19. In David L. Elliott, "An Interview with W. S. Merwin," 17.

20. That popular view is a distortion of Michelangelo's own idea, as expressed in his sonnet "Non ha l'ottimo artista alcun concetto": "No block of marble but it does not hide / the concept living in the artist's mind." *Michelangelo: Life, Letters, and Poetry,* trans. George Bull and Peter Porter (Oxford: Oxford University Press, 1987), 153.

21. *Asian Figures* (New York: Atheneum, 1973), no page number.

22. Elsewhere Merwin has said that this situation holds for all poetry: "The postphenomenologists [say] that there is no subject and that there is no need for a subject, that the poetry need have no relationship to any subject. The poem is on its own, apart from anything. Something that seems to me fairly obvious is that both things are true: the poem does exist on its own, but that doesn't mean the poem has no relation to a

subject. These two apparently contradictory things are actually happening at the same time. The poem is not the same thing as the subject. The poem would also not exist *without* the subject. The two have an essential relationship; and I really can't imagine being interested in a poem that doesn't have a subject, some kind of subject" (In Elliott, 17).

23. Richard Howard, "A Poetry of Darkness," *The Nation* 211:20 (14 December 1970): 634.

Chapter 2—Myth

1. (New Haven: Yale University Press, 1952): vii.

2. Mark Christhilf, *W. S. Merwin the Mythmaker,* 1–2.

3. Alice N. Benston, "Myth in the Poetry of W. S. Merwin," 180.

4. In David L. Elliott, "An Interview with W. S. Merwin," 3.

5. In David Applefield and Jelle Jeensma, "A Dialogue With W. S. Merwin," 76.

6. In Elliott, 3.

7. In Richard Jackson, "Unnaming the Myths," 48.

8. In Elliott, 3.

9. In Michael Pettit, "W. S. Merwin: An Interview," 9.

10. Anthony Libby, "W. S. Merwin and the Nothing That Is," in *Mythologies of Nothing: Mystical Death in American Poetry 1940–70* (Urbana: University of Illinois Press, 1984), 191.

11. *The Complete Poems 1927–1979* (New York: Farrar, Straus, Giroux, 1983), 139–42.

12. On the basis of a comparison to Miller Williams rather than to Elizabeth Bishop, David Baker arrives at a similar characterization of Merwin: "The conflict, as I see it, is . . . the conflict in America between Eliot [whom Merwin resembles] and Robinson [whom Williams resembles], or earlier between Emerson and Twain, even between Edwards and Franklin. It is probably traceable to the very deep, essential tension

between Platonic and Aristotelian inclinations—that is, to the most basic rift in Western thought" ("To Advantage Dressed: Miller Williams Among the Naked Poets," *The Southern Review* 26:4 [Autumn 1990]: 829).

13. Anthony Libby, "Angels in the Bone Shop," in *Learning the Trade: Essays on W. B. Yeats and Contemporary Poetry,* ed. Deborah Fleming (West Cornwall, Conn.: Locust Hill, 1993), 291.

14. Neal Bowers, "W. S. Merwin and Postmodern American Poetry," 249.

15. Randall Stiffler, "'The Annunciation' of W. S. Merwin," *Concerning Poetry* 16:2 (Fall 1983): 59.

16. Luke 1:35, New English Bible.

17. Kenneth Andersen, "The Poetry of W. S. Merwin," 279.

18. Stiffler, 58–59.

19. Cary Nelson, "The Resources of Failure: W. S. Merwin's Deconstructive Career," in *W. S. Merwin: Essays on the Poetry,* 85.

20. Yves Bonnefoy, *Mythologies,* vol. II, ed. Wendy Doniger, trans. Gerald Honigsblum et al. (Chicago: University of Chicago Press, 1991): 1046, 1108, 1191.

21. Academy of American Poets, 1968.

22. Andersen, 280.

23. Benston, 193.

24. "Contemporary Poetry and the Metaphors for the Poem," *Georgia Review* 32:2 (Summer 1978): 329–31.

25. "W. S. Merwin: Rational and Irrational Poetry," 309–10.

26. Contoski, 311.

27. Libby, "W. S. Merwin and the Nothing That Is," 192.

28. Baker, 818.

29. Contoski, 314.

30. Contoski, 320.

31. William Marling, "Indiscriminately Prolific Poet," 199.

Chapter 3—Apocalypse

1. Jim Harrison, "Homily," *The Theory & Practice of Rivers and New Poems* (Livingston, Mon.: Clark City Press, 1989): 34.

2. I have derived this idea of tragedy from Martha Nussbaum's excellent book *The Fragility of Goodness: Luck and Ethics in Greek Tragedy and Philosophy* (Cambridge: Cambridge University Press, 1986). Nussbaum writes: "That I am an agent, but also a plant; that much that I did not make goes toward making me whatever I shall be praised or blamed for being; that I must constantly choose among competing and apparently incommensurable goods and that circumstances may force me to a position in which I cannot help being false to something or doing some wrong; that an event that simply happens to me may, without my consent, alter my life; that it is equally problematic to entrust one's good to friends, lovers, or country and to try to have a good life without them—all these I take to be . . . the material of tragedy" (5).

3. Cheri Davis, *W. S. Merwin,* 38.

4. Alice N. Benston, "Myth in the Poetry of W. S. Merwin," 204.

5. Edward J. Brunner, *Poetry as Labor and Privilege,* 12.

6. Stephen Stepanchev, "W. S. Merwin," 110.

7. "The Road Not Taken," *The Poetry of Robert Frost* (New York: Holt, Rinehart and Winston, 1979), 105.

8. Paul Carroll, "The Spirit with Long Ears and Paws," in *The Poem in Its Skin* (Chicago: Big Table, 1968), 143–44.

9. Carroll, 144.

10. Carroll, 146–47.

11. Kenneth Andersen, "The Poetry of W. S. Merwin," 283.

12. Stephen Stepanchev, 119.

13. In Michael Pettit, "W. S. Merwin: An Interview," 15.

14. William V. Davis, "'Like the Beam of a Lightless Star,'" 45.

15. Ludwig Wittgenstein, *Culture and Value,* ed. G. H. von Wright, trans. Peter Winch (Chicago: University of Chicago Press, 1980), 18.

16. In Jack Myers and Michael Simms, "Possibilities of the Unknown," 171.

17. Daniel Hoffman, "Poetry: Schools of Dissidents," *Harvard Guide to Contemporary American Writing,* ed. Daniel Hoffman (Cambridge: Harvard University Press, 1979), 542. Many other commentators have noticed this pattern of recurring nouns. Jarold Ramsey points out that this vocabulary is more or less continuous through Merwin's corpus ("The Continuities of W. S. Merwin: 'What Has Escaped Us We Bring with Us," in Nelson and Folsom, 20). Charles Altieri says the recurrence of the terms "forces on the reader a sense that no specific instance of an image contains its complete meaning" (Nelson and Folsom, 178). Helen Vendler calls them "obsessive counters" that Merwin only manipulates vacuously ("W. S. Merwin," in *Part of Nature, Part of Us* [Cambridge: Harvard University Press, 1980], 235). Richard Howard says these "figures of force" gather experience "like filings in a magnetic field" and allow us to "track Merwin like a *moving target,* indeed" ("W. S. Merwin," 437).

18. He does use periods to end the sentences of "The Last One" in *The Lice,* and "The Archaic Maker" in *The Rain in the Trees.* But "The Archaic Maker" is in prose, and Merwin disavows the punctuation in "The Last One." When an interviewer noted that there was only one punctuated poem in *The Lice,* Merwin's reply was "*Is* there a punctuated poem?" Reminded of "The Last One," he replied, "Oh, I guess that poem is punctuated, yes, but it is not a conventional punctuation. It is a deliberate marking of the ends of the lines, which I could just as well have done with a dash or some other mark" (In Philip L. Gerber and Robert J. Gemmett, "'Tireless Quest,'" 17).

19. Cary Nelson, in Nelson and Folsom, 104.

20. Davis, "'Like the Beam of a Lightless Star,'" 46.

21. Edward J. Brunner, 107.

22. On page 100, Merwin devotes a lengthy paragraph to meditating on the stains in his father's church building.

23. John Vogelsang, "Toward the Great Language," 108.

24. Edward J. Brunner, 135.

25. Jarold Ramsey, in Nelson and Folsom, 22.

26. "Most of *The Lice* was written at a time when I really felt there was no point in writing. I got to the point where I thought the future was so bleak that there was no point in writing anything at all. And so the poems kind of pushed their way upon me when I wasn't thinking of writing. I would be out growing vegetables and walking around the countryside when all of a sudden I'd find myself writing a poem, and I'd write it" (In David L. Elliott, "An Interview with W. S. Merwin," 6).

Chapter 4—Ecology

1. Elias Canetti, *The Secret Heart of the Clock,* trans. Joel Agee (New York: Farrar Straus Giroux, 1989), 54.

2. In David L. Elliott, "An Interview with W. S. Merwin," 6.

3. *Microcosmos* (New York: Simon and Schuster, 1986), 228–29.

4. Margulis and Sagan, 195.

5. Margulis and Sagan, 227.

6. *The Sovereignty of Good* (New York: Ark, 1985). All three quotations are from page 84.

7. "Listening to Boredom," *Harper's* 290:1738 (March 1995): 13.

8. In Richard Jackson, "Unnaming the Myths," 49.

9. In Michael Clifton, "W. S. Merwin: An Interview," 21.

10. In David Applefield and Jelle Jeensma, "A Dialogue With W. S. Merwin," 74.

11. Ed Folsom, "'I Have Been a Long Time in a Strange Country': W. S. Merwin and America," in Nelson and Folsom, 239.

12. Folsom, in Nelson and Folsom, 239.

13. Folsom, in Nelson and Folsom, 240.

14. William H. Rueckert, "Rereading *The Lice:* A Journal," in Nelson and Folsom, 56.

15. *Poetry Reading by W. S. Merwin,* 11 November 1987, Modern Language Center, Harvard University.

16. George Oppen, "An Adequate Vision: From the Daybooks," ed. Michael Davidson, *Ironwood* 13:2 (Fall 1985): 13.

17. Jarold Ramsey, "The Continuities of W. S. Merwin: 'What Has Escaped Us We Bring with Us,'" in Nelson and Folsom, 33.

18. Ramsey, 33.

19. Anthony Libby, "W. S. Merwin and the Nothing That Is," in *Mythologies of Nothing: Mystical Death in American Poetry 1940–70* (Urbana: University of Illinois Press, 1984), 203.

20. Jan B. Gordon, "The Dwelling of Disappearance," 127.

21. Charles Altieri, "Situating Merwin's Poetry since 1970," in Nelson and Folsom, 184.

22. In Michael Clifton, "W. S. Merwin: An Interview," 22.

23. Anthony Libby, "Merwin's Planet: Alien Voices," 56.

24. Albert Camus, *The Myth of Sisyphus and Other Essays,* trans. Justin O'Brien (New York: Vintage, 1955), 13.

25. Edward J. Brunner, 146.

26. "Camping Out in Baja's Remotest Reaches," 60.

Chapter 5—Society

1. "A 'Courageous and Magnanimous Creation,'" *Harvard Review* 9 (Fall 1995): 107.

2. "The New Transcendentalism: The Visionary Strain in Merwin, Ashbery, and Ammons," in *Figures of Capable Imagination* (New York: Seabury Press, 1976), 127. Perloff, citing the same passage by Bloom, says, "One may want to quarrel with Bloom's list of legitimate precursors, but his prediction that the poet's 'litanies of denudation' would read oddly to the next generation has already come true" ("Apoca-

lypse Then: Merwin and the Sorrows of Literary History," in Nelson and Folsom, 125).

3. Though here Perloff would disagree, arguing that "the measured abstractions, the careful distancing in Merwin's poetry about war and suffering and loss" make his poetry sufficiently ornamental that even "readers of the *New Yorker,* coming across a poem like 'The Asians Dying' on a glossy page between those gorgeous ads for fur coats and diamonds and resorts in St. Croix, were not put off" ("Apocalypse Then," in Nelson and Folsom, 130, 141).

4. In Frank MacShane, "A Portrait of W. S. Merwin," 7.

5. Asked in an interview whether he reads Thoreau often, Merwin's reply was, "Well, I keep him in the john. He's been there for years. So I go back and read things over again. I think *Walden* is an incredible book. I feel grateful to Thoreau in a way. He's been a companion" (RM, 324).

6. Henry David Thoreau, *Walden,* ed. J. Lyndon Shanley (Princeton, N.J.: Princeton University Press, 1971), 3.

7. Thoreau, 14.

8. Edward J. Brunner, *Poetry as Labor and Privilege,* 155.

9. Quoted in Brunner, 154.

10. Brunner, 155.

11. Clifford Cobb, Ted Halstead, and Jonathan Rowe, "If the GDP Is Up, Why Is America Down?," *The Atlantic Monthly* 276:4 (October 1995): 65.

12. Cobb, et al., 72.

13. This group was identified as a distinct series by Ed Folsom, on whose perspicacious reading of *The Carrier of Ladders* I rely in what follows. See "Approaches and Removals: W. S. Merwin's Encounter with Whitman's America," *Shenandoah* 29:3 (Spring 2978): 57.

14. Folsom, "Approaches," 68.

15. Folsom, in Nelson and Folsom, 243.

16. Folsom, in Nelson and Folsom, 246.

17. Folsom, in Nelson and Folsom, 247.

18. Thomas B. Byers, "The Present Voices: W. S. Merwin since 1970," in Nelson and Folsom, 270.

Chapter 6—Love

1. Cary Nelson, "The Resources of Failure: W. S. Merwin's Deconstructive Career," in Nelson and Folsom, 113–15.

2. "The Struggle With Absence: Robert Creeley and W. S. Merwin," in *Enlarging the Temple: New Directions in American Poetry During the 1960s* (Lewisburg, Penn.: Bucknell University Press, 1979), 202.

3. William Marling places the blame on Merwin's simply writing too much, but his assessment of the quality of the poems matches that of Nelson and Altieri. Marling writes, "The love poems are mediocre. The longest of them, 'Kore,' which features a stanza for every letter of the Greek alphabet, has a few nice passages but is marred by lines such as 'The candles flutter in the stairs of your voice.' It becomes so tendentious that one is lucky to get past θ. The best of them, 'Islands,' seems like an homage to Circe of Kalypso, and hence of the old genre" ("Indiscriminately Prolific Poet," 200).

4. In David Applefield and Jelle Jeensma, "A Dialogue With W. S. Merwin," 76–77. Others have expressed similar views. For instance, Albert Camus has the narrator say in *The Plague* that ". . . love is never strong enough to find the words befitting it" (Trans. Stuart Gilbert [New York: Vintage, 1972]: 262).

5. Edward J. Brunner, *Poetry as Labor and Privilege,* 217.

6. In David L. Elliott, "An Interview with W. S. Merwin," 15.

7. A perfect example is catalog number 21 02 039, labeled "1965 Notes," a business envelope opened flat and covered with notes in just such stanzas separated by just such dashes.

8. C. Hugh Holman's *A Handbook to Literature* (Indianapolis: Bobbs-Merrill, 1980) defines the pathetic fallacy as "false emotionalism in writing resulting in a too impassioned description of nature. It is the carrying over to inanimate objects of the moods and passions of a human being." I do not mean to imply that using the pathetic fallacy is always bad (Shakespeare often uses it to good effect), but I do contend that this poem does not provide the dramatic context in which the pathetic fallacy could work.

9. *On Being Blue* (Boston: David R. Godine, 1976), 16–17.

10. There exist several accounts of the incident, among them Tom Clark, *The Great Naropa Poetry Wars* (Santa Barbara: Cadmus Editions, 1980), and Peter Marin, "Spiritual Obedience," *Harper's* 258: 1545 (February 1979): 43–58. In the latter, Merwin is not identified, but instead is referred to as "a well-known poet, P."

11. Friedrich Nietzsche, *Daybreak,* trans. R. J. Hollingdale (Cambridge: Cambridge University Press, 1982), 156–57.

12. "Hindsight, Insight, Foresight," *Poetry* 153:4 (January 1989): 239.

13. "Old Song," in *The Collected Poems of Robert Creeley: 1945–1975* (Berkeley: University of California Press, 1982), 41.

14. *Finding Losses* (New Rochelle, N.Y.: The Elizabeth Press, 1976), 46.

15. Ludwig Wittgenstein, *Culture and Value,* ed. G. H. von Wright, trans. Peter Winch (Chicago: University of Chicago Press, 1980), 33–34.

Chapter 7—Family

1. In Richard Jackson, "Unnaming the Myths," 49.

2. In David Applefield and Jelle Jeensma, "A Dialogue With W. S. Merwin," 76.

3. In Jackson, 51.

4. "The Continuities of W. S. Merwin: 'What Has Escaped Us We Bring With Us,'" in Nelson and Folsom, 35–36.

5. Ed Folsom, "'I Have Been a Long Time in a Strange Country,'" in Nelson and Folsom, 226.

6. In David L. Elliott, "An Interview with W. S. Merwin," 13.

7. "The Poetry of W. S. Merwin," 282.

8. "On First Looking into Chapman's Homer." Even Keats's Cortez is less a historical than a mythical figure, since after all it was Balboa who saw the Pacific from the isthmus of Darien. The historical Cortez saw Mexico City.

9. Philip L. Gerber and Robert J. Gemmett, "'Tireless Quest,'" 18.

10. Linda Trengen and Gary Storhoff, "Order and Energy in Merwin's *The Drunk in the Furnace,*" 49.

11. Trengen and Storhoff, 49.

12. *Poetry as Labor and Privilege,* 78–81. Brunner says, "when Merwin, in England, questioned his ancestors, he had no idea what answers he would receive if they had been able to reply," but "soon after Merwin was back in America he set about finding information that would in fact produce nothing but answers," after which he is "encumbered with knowledge" (78).

13. *Poetry as Labor and Privilege,* 81.

14. Charles Molesworth, for example, says, "*Unframed Originals,* one of the finest memoirs of any of the poets of his generation, may in fact be Merwin's single best book" ("W. S. Merwin: Style, Vision, Influence," in Nelson and Folsom, 145). Sven Birkerts writes that "*Unframed Originals* is Merwin's finest work, poetry included, and it gives the lie to what is the more strained lyricism of the poems and earlier prose" ("The Miner Surfaces: The Prose of W. S. Merwin," *Parnassus: Poetry in Review* 20:1&2 [1995]: 294).

15. Molesworth, 145.

16. Thomas B. Byers, "The Present Voices: W. S. Merwin since 1970," in Nelson and Folsom, 256.

17. *Human, All Too Human: A Book for Free Spirits,* trans. R. J. Hollingdale (Cambridge: Cambridge University Press, 1986), 150.

18. Exodus 20:5.

19. Matthew chapter 4.

20. Byers, in Nelson and Folsom, 264.

21. Byers, in Nelson and Folsom, 265.

22. Walter Kalaidjian, "Linguistic Mirages: Language and Landscape in Merwin's Later Poetry," in Nelson and Folsom, 214–15.

23. Brunner says, "All the themes in *Opening the Hand* are present in 'Yesterday': the difficulty of speech in an impossible situation . . . ; the need for a sympathetic auditor whose understanding will extend outward to a situation and encompass it without judgment; the necessity of suspending one's own claims in an effort to allow someone else to speak, and to hear the words of that person in all their clarity" (270).

Chapter 8—Hawaii

1. "Islands of Loss and Hope," *Sierra* 79:2 (March/April 1994): 116.

2. Elizabeth Royte, "On the Brink: Hawaii's Vanishing Species," *National Geographic* 188:3 (September 1995): 5. The information in this paragraph and the next is condensed from Royte's essay, and the other two quoted passages are from page 14.

3. "Sacred Bones," 21.

4. *Lyric Philosophy* (Toronto: University of Toronto Press, 1992), 222.

5. "Letters," 43.

6. In David L. Elliott, "An Interview with W. S. Merwin," 23.

7. In David Applefield and Jelle Jeensma, "A Dialogue With W. S. Merwin," 76.

8. "An Old Master and Four New Poets," *The Hudson Review* 41:4 (Winter 1989): 730.

9. "Living on an Island," 30.

10. "Living on an Island," 30.

11. In Elliott, 23.

12. "Living on an Island," 30.

13. "Aloha, Malathion," 235.

14. "Living on an Island," 29–30.

15. "Living on an Island," 30.

16. Judith Kitchen, "Skating on Paper," *The Georgia Review* 47:3 (Fall 1993): 585. Kitchen is talking about a different poem (indeed, she is talking about a different book, *Travels*), but her point holds in regard to this poem.

17. *Asian Figures,* 35.

Chapter 9—France

1. "'I Have Been a Long Time in a Strange Country': W. S. Merwin and America," in Nelson and Folsom, 232.

2. *Travels* is the text that brings about this revelation in Merwin. David St. John, reviewing *Travels,* says the poems in that book "often bear witness to the pursuit or revelation of nature's secrets, yet the wisdom borne by and born of these 'secrets' inevitably reflects one truth—that, after the travels we call our lives, we necessarily return to our true and final home, the natural world" ("Home at Last," *Los Angeles Times Book Review* [27 December 1992], 9). Although there are differences between Hawaii and France (Merwin built his home in the one but not the other, for example), Merwin can see now that what he was seeking in France was a sense of place and that France gave him exactly that, though only now is he prepared to name it.

3. "The Miner Surfaces: The Prose of W. S. Merwin," *Parnassus: Poetry in Review* 20:1&2 (1995): 285–95.

4. *The Complete Poetry and Prose of William Blake,* ed. David V. Erdman (New York: Anchor Books, 1988), 38.

5. Trans. Richmond Lattimore (Chicago: University of Chicago Press, 1951), 453.

6. *Culture and Value,* ed. G. H. von Wright, trans. Peter Winch (Chicago: University of Chicago Press, 1980), 77.

7. *The Poetry of Robert Frost,* ed. Edward Connery Lathem (New York: Holt, Rinehart and Winston, 1969), 348.

8. Although his sphere of concerns is very different from Merwin's, Peter Singer's arguments support Merwin's conclusions about the ill-treatment of animals caused by agribusiness farming methods. See *Animal Liberation* (New York: Avon, 1990).

9. Charles Altieri, "The Struggle With Absence: Robert Creeley and W. S. Merwin," in *Enlarging the Temple: New Directions in American Poetry During the 1960s* (Lewisburg, Penn.: Bucknell University Press, 1979), 199.

BIBLIOGRAPHY

Works by W. S. Merwin

Books of Poetry—Selected

A Mask for Janus. New Haven: Yale University Press, 1952.
The Dancing Bears. New Haven: Yale University Press, 1954.
Green with Beasts. New York: Alfred A. Knopf, 1956.
The Drunk in the Furnace. New York: Macmillan, 1960.
The Moving Target. New York: Atheneum, 1963.
The Lice. New York: Atheneum, 1967.
The Carrier of Ladders. New York: Atheneum, 1970.
Writings to an Unfinished Accompaniment. New York: Atheneum, 1973.
The Compass Flower. New York: Atheneum, 1977.
Finding the Islands. San Francisco: North Point, 1982.
Opening the Hand. New York: Atheneum, 1983.
Selected Poems. New York: Atheneum, 1988.
The Rain in the Trees. New York: Alfred A. Knopf, 1988.
Travels. New York: Alfred A. Knopf, 1993.
The Vixen. New York: Alfred A. Knopf, 1996.

Books of Prose

The Miner's Pale Children. New York: Atheneum, 1970.
Houses and Travellers. New York: Atheneum, 1977.
Unframed Originals. New York: Atheneum, 1982.
Regions of Memory: Uncollected Prose, 1949–82, ed. Ed Folsom and Cary Nelson. Urbana: University of Illinois Press, 1987.
The Lost Upland. New York: Alfred A. Knopf, 1992.

BIBLIOGRAPHY

Books of Translations—Selected

The Poem of the Cid. New York: Las Americas, 1959.

The Satires of Persius. Bloomington: Indiana University Press, 1961.

Selected Translations: 1948–1968. New York: Atheneum, 1968.

Follain, Jean. *Transparence of the World.* New York: Atheneum, 1969.

Asian Figures. New York: Atheneum, 1973.

Neruda, Pablo. *Twenty Love Poems and a Song of Despair.* New York: Penguin, 1976.

Sanskrit Love Poetry. New York: Columbia University Press, 1977. Translated with J. Moussaieff Masson. Later reprinted as *The Peacock's Egg.* San Francisco: North Point, 1981.

Euripides. *Iphigenia at Aulis.* New York: Oxford University Press, 1978. Translated with George E. Dimock, Jr.

Selected Translations: 1968–1978. New York: Atheneum, 1979.

From the Spanish Morning. New York: Atheneum, 1985.

Vertical Poetry. Roberto Juarroz. San Francisco: North Point, 1988.

Voices: Aphorisms by Antonio Porchia. Revised and Enlarged Edition. New York: Alfred A. Knopf, 1988.

Recordings—Selected

Conversation with Richard Howard. Academy of American Poets, 1968. An introductory lecture on poetry by Howard, followed by a reading by Merwin of poems from his first six books, interspersed with discussion by the poets.

Education of a Poet. Howard Norman and W. S. Merwin. Academy of American Poets, 1982. Two discussions, one by Norman and one by Merwin, on oral traditions. Merwin's part consists largely of his reading and discussing poems he has translated from oral traditions into written English.

BIBLIOGRAPHY

New Letters on the Air, 1979. A recording of a public reading.

New Letters on the Air, 1993. An interview.

Poetry Reading by W. S. Merwin, 11 November 1987. Modern Language Center, Harvard University. A recording of a public reading.

W. S. Merwin. Lannan Literary Videos #3, 1989. A video combining an interview and a reading of poems from *Selected Poems* and *The Rain in the Trees.*

W. S. Merwin Reading His Poetry. New York: Caedmon (HarperCollins), 1992. Recorded in 1970. Includes poems from *Green with Beasts, The Drunk in the Furnace, The Moving Target, The Lice,* and *The Carrier of Ladders.*

Essays and Nonfiction—Selected

"The Religious Poet," in *A Casebook on Dylan Thomas,* ed. John M. Brinnin (New York: Crowell, 1960), 59–67. Reprinted from *Adam International Review* 238 (1953): 73–78. An essay praising Dylan Thomas as a religious poet, on the grounds that in his poetry the human imagination is "for him the image of the divine imagination."

"Aloha, Malathion: Hawaii Wakes Up to Pesticides," *The Nation* 240:8 (2 March 1985): 235–37. A report on a Department of Agriculture plan to spray the Hawaiian islands with pesticides: 108–156 sprayings, using six different chemicals, over a period of six years.

"Listening to Wyatt," *American Poetry Review* 18:2 (March/April 1989): 51–54. Merwin's introduction to his own selection of Wyatt's poems. Argues that Wyatt's irregular rhythms contribute to the music of his poems.

"The Sacred Bones of Maui," *New York Times Magazine* 138 (6 August 1989): 21–35. Narrates the controversy surrounding a developer's plan to build a large hotel on the site of an ancient burial ground.

"Letters," *American Poetry Review* 19:2 (March/April 1990): 43–45. An appeal to readers to support the protest of government-sanctioned

BIBLIOGRAPHY

destruction of the Wao Kele O Puna rain forest, then the largest intact lowland rain forest in the Hawaiian islands.

"The Wake of the Blackfish: A Memoir of George Kirstein," *The Paris Review* 32:115 (Summer 1990): 267–315. Recollections from Merwin's long friendship with the former owner of *The Nation,* reflecting Merwin's long-standing interest in the sea.

"Camping Out in Baja's Remotest Reaches," *New York Times Magazine* 140 (3 March 1991): 50–60. A description of a group camping trip and a lament for the damage human activity inflicts on the local ecosystem, especially the fish and birds.

"Living on an Island," *Sierra* 76:5 (September/October 1991): 29–30. A brief statement about why he lives in Hawaii.

"Snail Song," *Sierra* 79:2 (March/April 1994): 110–17. Tells how Europeans and Americans have destroyed most species indigenous to the Hawaiian islands and replaced them with species imported from elsewhere; uses as its focal illustration the diminishing numbers and varieties of Hawaiian land snails.

Interviews—Selected

Applefield, David, and Jelle Jeensma. "A Dialogue With W. S. Merwin." *Frank* 13 (Winter/Spring 1991): 72–77. Condensed from two interviews, this brief exchange focuses almost exclusively on Merwin's ecological concerns.

Clifton, Michael. "W. S. Merwin: An Interview." *American Poetry Review* 12:4 (July/August 1983): 17–22. Emphasizes the transition in Merwin's work from metrical to "open form" and the causes of Merwin's pessimism about the human condition.

Elliott, David L. "An Interview with W. S. Merwin." *Contemporary Literature* 29:1 (Spring 1988): 1–25. Concentrates on the differences between Merwin's work in the 1960s, especially *The Lice,* and his later work, emphasizing the effects of his recent attention to the Pacific region.

Gerber, Philip L., and Robert J. Gemmett. "'Tireless Quest': A Conversation with W. S. Merwin." *The English Record* 19:3 (Feb. 1969): 9–18. A useful interview focused on the transition from *The Drunk in the Furnace* to *The Moving Target* and *The Lice.*

Jackson, Richard. "Unnaming the Myths." In *Acts of Mind: Conversations with Contemporary Poets.* University: The University of Alabama Press, 1983. 48–52. Discusses poems that would later be collected into *Opening the Hand,* with emphasis on issues of myth, perception, and language.

Myers, Jack, and Michael Simms. "Possibilities of the Unknown: Conversations with W. S. Merwin." *Southwest Review* 68:2 (Spring 1983): 164–80. A public interview that includes some dialogue with audience members, attending to the personal and political motivations of Merwin's writing, with emphasis on *The Lice* and Merwin's translations.

Pettit, Michael. "W. S. Merwin: An Interview." *Black Warrior Review* 8:2 (Spring 1982): 7–20. A focused interview, concentrating on the role and importance of language.

Works about Merwin

Books

Brunner, Edward J. *Poetry as Labor and Privilege: The Writings of W. S. Merwin.* Urbana: University of Illinois Press, 1991. An illuminating and thorough chronological overview of Merwin's work through *The Rain in the Trees,* with special attention to what his unpublished and uncollected works reveal about his published work. By far the best book on Merwin to date.

BIBLIOGRAPHY

Christhilf, Mark. *W. S. Merwin the Mythmaker.* Columbia: University of Missouri Press, 1986. A one-dimensional treatment of Merwin as the creator of his own myth, treating the poetry through *Opening the Hand* but with heavy emphasis on the books through *Writings to an Unfinished Accompaniment.*

Davis, Cheri. *W. S. Merwin.* Boston: Twayne, 1981. A treatment of the books through *The Compass Flower,* including some discussion of the translations and early prose, marred by too reverent an approach that sometimes weakens the analysis.

Hoeppner, Edward Haworth. *Echoes and Moving Fields: Structure and Subjectivity in the Poetry of W. S. Merwin and John Ashbery.* Lewisburg, Penn.: Bucknell University Press, 1994. Compares Merwin and John Ashbery to show that their suppositions about, and patterns of, language shape their understanding of the possibilities and obligations of humans.

Nelson, Cary, and Ed Folsom. *W. S. Merwin: Essays on the Poetry.* Urbana: University of Illinois Press, 1987. A substantial and diverse collection; includes a description of the Merwin manuscript archive at the University of Illinois, reproductions of several typescript pages, and an extensive bibliography.

Articles, Reviews, and Parts of Books—Selected

Andersen, Kenneth. "The Poetry of W. S. Merwin." *Twentieth Century Literature* 16:4 (October 1970): 278–86. Argues that in Merwin's first five books the significant changes from volume to volume constitute a coherent philosophy grounded in "a vital, changing point of view."

Atlas, James. "Diminishing Returns: The Writings of W. S. Merwin." In *American Poetry Since 1960: Some Critical Perspectives.* Ed. Robert Shaw. Cheshire: Carcanet Press, 1973. 69–81. Argues that Merwin's poems, in spite of his auspicious beginnings and his

BIBLIOGRAPHY

successful translations, became weaker rather than stronger through *The Carrier of Ladders,* then the most recent volume.

Benston, Alice N. "Myth in the Poetry of W. S. Merwin." In *Poets in Progress.* Ed. Edward Hungerford. Evanston, Ill.: Northwestern University Press, 1967. 179–204. A reading of the first four books. Benston argues that Merwin's use of myth enables him to confront mystery as a universal human problem without trying to eliminate it by a reductive, doctrinaire belief system.

Bowers, Neal. "W. S. Merwin and Postmodern American Poetry." *Sewanee Review* 98:2 (Spring 1990): 246–59. To explain Merwin's importance, this article points to his persistent search for form and his independence from standard cliques and categories.

Byers, Thomas B. "W. S. Merwin: A Description of Darkness." In *What I Cannot Say: Self, Word, and World in Whitman, Stevens, and Merwin.* Urbana: University of Illinois Press, 1989. 79–110. Contrasts Merwin's poetry, especially *The Lice,* with Walt Whitman's *Leaves of Grass,* demonstrating that Merwin is more skeptical than Whitman about poetry's ability to unite us with each other and to nature.

Contoski, Victor. "W. S. Merwin: Rational and Irrational Poetry." *Literary Review: An International Journal of Contemporary Writing* 22:3 (Spring 1979): 309–20. Defends Merwin's poetry against charges of obscurity and irrationality and shows its affinities with medieval ideals of the moral journey.

Davis, William V. "'Like the Beam of a Lightless Star': The Poetry of W. S. Merwin." *Poet & Critic* 14:1 (1982): 45–56. Demonstrates the thematic continuity in Merwin's poetry through *Writings to an Unfinished Accompaniment,* in contrast to the frequent bracketing off of the first four books.

Frawley, William. "Merwin's Unpunctuated Verse." *Notes on Contemporary Literature* 7:4 (September 1977): 2–3. An article the tiny size of which belies its explanatory power. Frawley argues that Merwin

BIBLIOGRAPHY

is able to write coherent verse without punctuation because of his reliance on a particular grammatical construction: adverbial prepositional phrases.

Gordon, Jan B. "The Dwelling of Disappearance: W. S. Merwin's *The Lice.*" *Modern Poetry Studies* 3:3 (1972): 119–38. Argues that Merwin's poetry inhabits a universe without objects and therefore without subject/object relations.

Howard, Richard. "W. S. Merwin: 'We Survived the Selves That We Remembered.'" In *Alone With America: Essays on the Art of Poetry in the United States Since 1950.* Enlarged Edition. New York: Atheneum, 1980. 412–49. Contends, in Howard's inimitable florid prose, that Merwin's poetry "has moved from preterition to presence to prophecy."

Kyle, Carol. "A Riddle for the New Year: Affirmation in W. S. Merwin." *Modern Poetry Studies* 4:3 (Winter 1973): 288–303. In spite of its reputation for gloomy pessimism, *The Lice,* according to Kyle, is an affirmative book that rejoices in the staying power of the spirit.

Lazer, Hank. "For a Coming Extinction: A Reading of W. S. Merwin's *The Lice.*" *ELH* 49:1 (Spring 1982): 262–85. Describes *The Lice* as a "planetary elegy" that laments human destructiveness and shortsightedness and that seeks individual integration in the face of time's fragmentation.

Libby, Anthony. "Merwin's Planet: Alien Voices." *Criticism* 24:1 (Winter 1982): 48–63. Discusses the meaning of Merwin's propensity for speaking through animals in his poems. Libby compares "Merwin's planet" to the science fiction that was popular at the time of Merwin's middle books.

MacShane, Frank. "A Portrait of W. S. Merwin." *Shenandoah* 21:2 (Winter 1970): 3–14. Part personal reminiscence and part discussion of the poems, this essay includes some interesting passages quoted from Merwin's letters.

BIBLIOGRAPHY

Marling, William. "Indiscriminately Prolific Poet." *Southwest Review* 63:2 (Spring 1978): 198–202. Considers *The Compass Flower* and *Houses and Travellers* examples of a tendency in Merwin to include too much weak work in his books.

McCorkle, James. "W. S. Merwin's Poetics of Memory." In *The Still Performance: Writing, Self, and Interconnection in Five Postmodern American Poets.* Charlottesville: University Press of Virginia, 1989. 130–70. Argues that Merwin's poetry inclines toward silence but that memory saves it from silence by provisionally recovering what has been lost and providing therefore a connection to the world.

Peters, Robert. "The Great American Poetry Bake-Off: or, Why W. S. Merwin Wins All Those Prizes." In *The Great American Poetry Bake-Off.* Metuchen, N.J.: The Scarecrow Press, 1979. 258–68. A brilliant cautionary essay in response to *Writings to an Unfinished Accompaniment,* identifying tendencies toward formula and shallowness in Merwin's poetry.

Stepanchev, Stephen. "W. S. Merwin." In *American Poetry Since 1945.* New York: Harper and Row, 1965. 107–23. Argues that, in spite of its drastic formal changes, the themes in *The Moving Target* are continuous with those of Merwin's first four books.

Trengen, Linda, and Gary Storhoff. "Order and Energy in Merwin's *The Drunk in the Furnace.*" *Concerning Poetry* 13:1 (Spring 1980): 47–52. An excellent essay that sees Merwin depicting a static, conventional society through most of the book, then testing that society by the chaotic energy of the title character.

Vogelsang, John. "Toward the Great Language: W. S. Merwin." *Modern Poetry Studies* 3:3 (1972): 97–118. Reads Merwin's poetry through *The Carrier of Ladders* as an ongoing attempt to write "the great language" of transcendence Merwin imagines in his "Notes for a Preface."

INDEX

This index does not include references to material in the notes.

Altieri, Charles, 91
apocalypse, 15, 43–59, 60–64, 74–76, 86, 136
ars poetica, 5, 10–22
Auden, W. H., 2, 4, 23
Augustine, 105

Baker, David, 41
Bartram, William, 76, 83
Basho, 98
Berryman, John, 2
Bible, 8, 9, 14, 26, 29–36, 48, 69, 114, 116, 128
Birkerts, Sven, 142–43, 146
Bishop, Elizabeth, 25
Blackmur, R. P., 2
Blake, William, 36, 143–44
Bloom, Harold, 74–75, 100
Bly, Robert, 5
Brodsky, Joseph, 63
Bronk, William, 104
Brunner, Edward J., 110
Buddhism, 4

Camus, Albert, 70
Christhilf, Mark, 42
confession, 105–6
Contoski, Victor, 39–41
Cook, James, 124

Corn, Alfred, 101
Creeley, Robert, 6, 103

Darwin, Charles, 61
Davis, William V., 57
Donne, John, 134

ecology, 16, 60–73

family, 105–23
Ferry, Dorothy Jeanne, 2
Folsom, Ed, 140
Ford, Harry, 4
France, 3, 21, 140–57
free verse, 6–7
Freud, Sigmund, 94
Frost, Robert, 148

Gass, William, 99
Glück, Louise, 5
Graves, Robert, 2

Hall, Donald, 5
Havel, Václav, 74
Hawaii, 4, 20, 114, 124–39, 140–41
Herrick, Robert, 103
Hodgson, Moira, 4
Homer, 5, 25–26, 145–47
Horace, 5
Howard, Richard, 36

INDEX

Jackson, Andrew, 76, 84
Jarman, Mark, 129

Kant, Immanuel, 9, 100
Keats, John, 109, 127–28
Kennedy, John F., 133

Lacan de Loubressac, 3
love, 17–19, 90–104

Margulis, Lynn, 60–62
Marling, William, 42
Marvell, Andrew, 96–97, 103
Merwin, Hanson, 117–18
Merwin, W. S.: autobiography, 105–23; career, 1–4; as a moral poet, 1, 8–10, 41–42; poetic development, 3, 14–15, 19; tragic vision, 43–47, 61, 90–92, 100, 124
Books:
    Asian Figures, 18
    The Carrier of Ladders, 4, 13, 16–17, 33, 39, 55, 74–90, 106–7, 114, 140
    The Compass Flower, 12, 17, 23, 42, 58, 86–104,140
    The Dancing Bears, 3, 11–13, 33, 92
    The Drunk in the Furnace, 14, 39–40, 107–10
    Finding the Islands, 18–19, 90, 92–93, 97–104, 116
    Green with Beasts, 13–14, 24–38, 147
    The Lice, 4, 11, 12, 13, 15–16, 19, 33, 39, 54–59, 60–75, 78, 84, 90, 100, 110, 114, 126, 136, 138, 148, 155
    The Lost Upland, 140–57
    A Mask for Janus, 2, 10–13, 23, 44–45
    The Miner's Pale Children, 154

Merwin, W. S.: Books *(continued)*

The Moving Target, 3, 4, 14–17, 35–36, 43–59, 66, 91, 108–10, 116–18, 126, 131, 136, 148, 153

Opening the Hand, 2, 12, 19, 114, 119–24, 140

The Rain in the Trees, 13, 19–20, 33, 101–4, 123, 124, 127–40

Regions of Memory, 2, 4, 6–10, 59, 62, 110–12, 140

Travels, 20–21, 54, 114, 116, 118, 123, 124, 131

Unframed Originals, 6, 19, 46, 57, 105–6, 110–19, 142

The Vixen, 21–22, 123, 140–57

Writings to an Unfinished Accompaniment, 17, 37–42, 128

Essays and Fiction:

"Affable Irregular: Recollections of R. P. Blackmur," 2

"Blackbird's Summer," 151–52

"Foie Gras," 144

"From a Mammon Card," 154

"La Pia," 116–17

"Mary," 46, 114–16

"Notes for a Preface," 59

"On Being Awarded the Pulitzer Prize," 4

"On Open Form," 6–10

"On the Bestial Floor," 62

"Shepherds," 145–51

"Tomatoes," 112–14

Poems:

"After Fires," 156

"Air," 15

"The Annunciation," 29–34

"Another Year Come," 52

"Apparitions," 121–22

"At the Same Time," 128

"Before Us," 102–4

INDEX

"Being Early," 101–2
"Berryman," 2
"Bread," 40
"Burning the Cat," 147
"Chord," 127–28
"City," 86–87
"The Cold Before the Moonrise," 15
"Cover Note," 20–21
"Crossing Place," 17
"The Crossroads of the World Etc.," 54–56
"The Current," 37
"The Day Itself," 116
"Death of a Favorite Bird," 70
"Dictum: For a Masque of Deluge," 44–45
"The Drunk in the Furnace," 110
"Empty Water," 132
"Envoy from D'Aubigné," 79–80
"The Eyes of the Drowned Watch Keels Going Over," 36–38
"Fly," 70, 100
"Fog-Horn," 14
"For a Coming Extinction," 19, 67–70
"For a Dissolving Music," 10–11
"The Forbears," 106–7
"Forgotten Streams," 152–53
"For Now," 57–59, 66
"For the Anniversary of My Death," 57
"For the Grave of Posterity," 56
"The Gardens of Zuñi," 83–84
"Grandfather in the Old Men's Home," 109–10
"Grandmother Dying," 110
"Habits," 40

INDEX

Merwin, W. S.: Poems *(continued)*
    "Home for Thanksgiving," 33, 46–47, 50, 109
    "Homeland," 84–85
    "The Houses," 120–21
    "Immortelles," 118
    "In Autumn," 71
    "The Inevitable Lightness," 131
    "Invocation," 14–15
    "Islands," 101–2
    "John Otto,"108–9
    "The Judgment of Paris," 33
    "Kore," 93–96, 98
    "Lackawanna," 82–83
    "The Last One," 33, 64–66, 70, 136, 138, 148
    "Legacies," 154–56
    "Lemuel's Blessing," 47–50, 109
    "Leviathan," 25–27
    "Looking for Mushrooms at Sunrise," 73
    "Losing a Language," 130–31, 152
    "Memory of Spring," 16–17
    "Mist," 40–41
    "The Mountains," 100
    "My Brothers the Silent," 72
    "Native," 133
    "Native Trees," 33, 129–30
    "Noah's Raven," 35–36, 47, 50
    "Now and Again," 52
    "The Oars," 119–20
    "Odysseus," 39–40
    "On the Subject of Poetry," 11–13, 21
    "Other Travellers to the River," 83

"Passing," 156–57
"Place," 136
"Possessions," 154–56
"Present," 141–42
"Presidents," 76
"The Prodigal Son," 33–36
"Proteus," 33
"Provision," 100
"Psalm: Our Fathers," 85–86
"Questions to Tourists Stopped by a Pineapple Field," 125–26
"Rain at Night," 137–39
"Road," 18
"The Rock," 87
"A Scale in May," 13, 67, 98
"Second Sight," 52–53
"Sestina," 12–13
"The Ships Are Made Ready in Silence," 51–52
"Signs," 98
"Song of Man Chipping an Arrowhead," 17
"The Sound of the Light," 13
"Sound of Rapids of Laramie River in Late August," 18
"Spring Equinox Full Moon," 96–97
"St. Vincent's," 87–89
"Standards," 46
"Strawberries," 120
"Sunset Water," 119–20
"Talking," 19
"Things," 153
"To Dana with the Gift of a Calendar," 18–19, 98–99
"To Dido," 13, 20
"To My Brother Hanson," 118

Merwin, W. S.: Poems *(continued)*
    "Travelling," 39–40
    "Turning to You," 99–100
    "Under the Migrants," 41
    "Vixen," 21–22
    "Vocations," 53–54
    "The Waving of a Hand," 120
    "The Way to the River," 91
    "The Wheels of the Trains," 82
    "When I Came from Colchis," 92
    "When You Go Away," 11
    "White Goat, White Ram," 27–28
    "The Widow," 66–67
    "Witness," 19–20, 130
    "Words from a Totem Animal," 13
    "Yesterday," 122–23

Michelangelo, 17
Milroy, Dido, 2, 4
Molesworth, Charles, 38
Murdoch, Iris, 63
myth, 13, 23–42, 43–44, 93–96, 105–6, 147

Naone, Dana, 4
The Nation, 3
Nietzsche, Friedrich, 9
Nixon, Richard, 76

Odysseus, 15, 38–42
open form, 6–10, 16, 44

INDEX

Perloff, Marjorie, 74–75, 100
Persephone, 93
Plato, 8, 9–10, 19
Poe, Edgar Allan, 5
Powell, John Wesley, 83
Pulitzer Prize, 4, 76
punctuation, 15–16, 54

Ramsey, Jarold, 106
Reagan, Ronald, 77
Rilke, Rainer Maria, 5
Rousseau, Jean-Jacques, 105

Sagan, Dorian, 60–62
Schwartz, Paula, 4
Shakespeare, William, 97
Smart, Christopher, 48
Snyder, Gary, 85
society, 16, 74–89
Socrates, 8, 36
Stiffler, Randall, 31

Tate, James, 69
Thoreau, Henry David, 77–78, 140–41, 156
Turner, Frederick Jackson, 83

war, 16–17, 39–40, 76
Whitman, Walt, 44, 65, 81
Wittgenstein, Ludwig, 51, 104, 147

Zwicky, Jan, 126